What Really Matters in Spelling

Research-Based Strategies and Activities

Patricia M. Cunningham

Wake Forest University

PEARSON

Boston   Columbus   Indianapolis   New York   San Francisco   Upper Saddle River
Amsterdam   Cape Town   Dubai   London   Madrid   Milan   Munich   Paris   Montreal   Toronto
Delhi   Mexico City   Sao Paulo   Sydney   Hong Kong   Seoul   Singapore   Taipei   Tokyo

Editor-in-Chief: Aurora Martínez Ramos
Editorial Assistant: Meagan French
Marketing Manager: Danae April
Production Editor: Annette Joseph
Editorial Production Service: Lynda Griffiths
Manufacturing Buyer: Megan Cochran
Electronic Composition: Denise Hoffman
Interior Design: Denise Hoffman
Art Director: Linda Knowles

10 9 8 7 6 5 4 3 2 1   RRD-VA   15 14 13 12 11

    www.pearsonpd.com

ISBN-10:   0-13-261222-4
ISBN-13:   978-0-13-261222-7

Contents

Preface

Spelling is one area of the elementary school curriculum that hasn't changed much in the last 200 years. On Mondays, in classrooms across the country, children are given a list of words to study. For homework throughout the week, they do activities intended to help them practice the words. They write the words five times each, put the words in sentences and in alphabetical order, and often write definitions for the words. On Fridays, millions of children take the spelling test. Some children get high grades on the spelling test week after week, and some children get low grades week after week. These spelling routines are so much a part of our experience and our parents' experiences and our grandparents' experiences that we seldom stop to question how effective they are. But we *should* question these practices because many children who complete these activities week after week, year after year, never become good spellers. Even some students who do well on weekly tests do not transfer those skills to their writing and may misspell the very same word when writing on Friday afternoon that they spelled correctly on the test on Friday morning.

Why do some students become good spellers and others remain poor spellers? Many veteran teachers admit to harboring the suspicion that it is not really all the practice and the tests that are creating the good spellers. Good spellers are usually strong visual learners. For these lucky students with strong visual memories, spelling words is easy. They remember how things—including words—look. Other students who have auditory or kinesthetic strengths but lack strong visual memories find it very difficult to learn the spelling of words or will learn them for the test and then quickly forget them.

The activities in this book are based in the psychological theory of pattern detection. Simply put, people learn new things by noticing new features and comparing them to things they already know. When seeing a grapefruit for the first time, a child who knows what an orange is will often dub the grapefruit "big orange." When encountering a miniature dog, a toddler is apt to call this tiny dog a "kitty" and is quite astonished when the dog begins to bark instead of meow. Noticing patterns—similarities and differences among things—is the basic mechanism the human brain has for learning new things.

Words have patterns too and these patterns are combinations of letters. For short words, the most important pattern in English words is the rhyme. Young children whose favorite books are Dr. Seuss books begin to notice that words that rhyme often have the same combinations of letters. They laugh as they learn that some fish are "sad" and "bad" and "glad" and are instructed to go ask their "dad" if they want to know why. Later they meet Mr. Gump who rides a "wump" with a "hump" that can "jump" and go "bump."

Bigger words also have patterns. These patterns are more complex but they are there to be discovered by anyone with an inquiring mind. Many children get tricycles for their fourth birthday, bicycles for their seventh, and are hoping for motorcycles for their sixteenth. *Fourth, sixth,* and *sixteenth* (and many other ordinal numbers) all share the pattern of adding the *t-h* to the number to show order. Cycle is the root word in *bicycle, tricycle,* and *motorcycle.* Later they may notice other patterns these words share when they learn about bipeds, binoculars, and binomials; tripods, triangles, and Triceratops; and motorize, motorcade, and motorist.

Good spellers have good visual memories because they notice the patterns in new words and compare them to the patterns in words they can already spell. A child who notices that *stray* is like *stay* but with an added *r* and that *portion* has that same "funny spelling" at the end as *action* and *motion* does not have to study these new words long in order to remember them forever. The activities in *What Really Matters in Spelling* are designed to turn all your students into "word detectives" who sleuth out patterns in words and use them to solve spelling mysteries.

Chapter 1 provides you with a fuller understanding of how good spellers use patterns to spell words as well as the research that underlies the pattern approach to spelling. In Chapter 2, you will learn to use a word wall to teach 100 key words that will unlock the spelling of thousands of words.

Chapter 3 describes a year's worth of instruction aimed at teaching children how to spell the words they most frequently encounter as they read and write. In addition, the chapter includes key words for all the common beginning consonants, blends, and digraphs and the most common rhyming patterns. The lessons in Chapter 3 will also teach your students how to spell words that end in *s, ed,* and *ing* and that people's names begin with capital letters. The key words and activities in this chapter are appropriate for first-graders and for older children who struggle with literacy or who are just learning to read in English.

In Chapter 4, students learn to spell another 100 key words that include the remaining high-frequency words and rhyming patterns. They also learn to spell the most common contractions and homophones, learn spelling changes needed when endings are added to words, and learn that place names, holidays, and days of the week begin with capital letters. The key words and activities in Chapter 4 are appropriate for students reading at second- and early third-grade levels, including older students whose literacy skills are not at grade level.

After they have become automatic at spelling the most common words and using the common spelling patterns, students are ready to develop more sophisticated spelling skills. Chapter 5 contains 100 key words and activities that will help your students develop a visual checking sense to determine which of two possible spelling patterns looks right. They also learn spellings and meanings for common homophones and compound words and that the names of months begin with a capital letter. Activities and key words in Chapter 5 are most appropriate for students of any age who read at the third- or fourth-grade level.

Chapter 6 focuses exclusively on polysyllabic words and the complex morphological system in which prefixes and suffixes are added to root words. Students will learn to spell 100 multisyllabic key words and how these key words can unlock the meaning, pronunciation, and spelling of hundreds of other words. The key words and activities in this chapter are appropriate for students in the upper elementary and middle grades whose reading level is at least fifth grade. Many high school students who struggle with reading or are becoming fluent in English could also benefit from a "crash course" in multisyllabic words based on the activities in Chapter 6.

As you read this book and think about the instruction and activities, ask yourself some "Does it make sense?" questions. Does it make sense that children would learn to spell words in the same way they learn everything else—by comparing new things to things they already know? Does it make sense that you can multiply the spelling power of your students by teaching them to spell a smaller number of key words and how to use these key words to spell hundreds of other words? Does it make sense that when children learn to spell by noticing patterns they will retain the spelling of the words better than if they just memorized the spelling of each word? Finally, does it make sense to continue teaching spelling in the traditional "list-Friday-test" way which, for generations, has failed with children who are not naturally good spellers?

New! CourseSmart eTextbook Available

CourseSmart is an exciting new choice for educators looking to save money. As an alternative to purchasing the printed textbook, educators can purchase an electronic version of the same content. With a CourseSmart eTextbook, educators can search the text, make notes online, print out reading assignments that incorporate lecture notes, and bookmark important passages for later review. For more information, or to purchase access to the CourseSmart eTextbook, visit www.coursesmart.com.

The **What Really Matters** *Series*

The past decade or so has seen a dramatic increase in the interest in what the research says about reading instruction. Much of this interest was stimulated by several recent federal education programs: the Reading Excellence Act of 1998, the No Child Left Behind Act of 2001, and the Individuals with Disabilities Education Act of 2004. The commonality shared by these federal laws is that each law restricts the use of federal funds to instructional services and support that have been found to be effective through "scientific research."

In this new series we bring you the best research-based instructional advice available. In addition, we have cut through the research jargon and at least some of the messiness and provide plain-language guides for teaching students to read and write. Our focus is helping you use the research as you plan and deliver instruction to your students. Our goal is that your lessons be as effective as we know how, given the research that has been published.

Our aim is that all children become active and engaged readers and writers and that all develop the proficiencies needed to be strong independent readers and writers. Each of the short books in this series features what we know about one aspect of teaching and learning to read and write independently. Each of these pieces is important to this goal but none is more important than the ultimate goal: active, strong, independent readers and writers who read and write eagerly.

So, enjoy these books and teach your students all to read and write.

Chapter 1

Spelling Matters

Are you a good speller? If you are, you can spell thousands of words—many more than the words you memorized for spelling lists during elementary school.

If you are a good speller, you can spell words you have never spelled before and even words you have never seen. How would you spell the word that means people who blog? What addiction would people have if they spent so much time blogging, they couldn't get their work done or get enough sleep? What word would you use to describe people who have a phobia about blogging?

If your brain spelled these blogging-related words—*bloggers, blogaholics,* and *blogophobic*—you have proved to yourself that you can spell words you have never spelled before—and certainly never studied and taken a test on. You can spell these new words because to be a good speller your brain has learned to notice and pay attention to patterns in words. People who dig are diggers, people who mug others are muggers, people who jog are joggers so you automatically double the *g* to spell the word *bloggers.* Your brain has taken the words you know how to spell—*diggers, muggers, joggers*—and figured out the pattern. If in the future our language develops some other new words such as *clin, stip,* and *strad,* you would automatically be able to spell the people who do these new actions—clinners, stippers, and stradders. You would also be able to spell the addictions and phobias these actions might lead to. People who clinned, stipped, and stradded excessively would be called clinaholics, stipaholics, and strataholics, and those who feared these actions would be clinaphobic, stipaphobic, and strataphobic.

Noticing the patterns in words is essential to being a good speller, but it is not the only thing you must do. Imagine that I asked you to spell the word that names the person who creates plays, would you spell that word playwrite or playwright? If you had never seen this word before, *playwrite* would be the logical choice—a person who writes plays should be a playwrite. If *playwrite* did not look right to you and you chose *playwright,* you have probably seen the word *playwright* before and may even have it filed in your brain along with other words in which *wright* means a person who makes or designs something, such as *millwright* and *wheelwright.*

English words are spelled based on patterns, but for many rhymes, there are two or more possible patterns. As you were learning words—perhaps very early when you were reading a Dr. Seuss book such as *Fox in Socks,* your brain started noticing the two possible patterns and began filing all the new words you saw under the correct pattern. If we could peer into your orthographic word store—that's the place in your brain where you store spelling patterns—we would see many patterns with just one spelling:

<u>at</u>:   at bat flat chat acrobat thermostat

<u>ing</u>:   sing wing cling string earring wingding

We would also see some rhymes sorted into two or three patterns:

<u>ight</u>:   fight slight bright moonlight eyesight

<u>ite</u>:   bite kite quite trite excite termite

These multiple pattern lists would also include some homophones—perhaps with a meaning clue your brain inserted so you could tell them apart

sight (eyes); site (place)   right (correct); write (pen)

If you are a good speller, you notice the spelling pattern in new words you encounter and then sort these words in your brain according to pattern. When you see a new word, you put it with the ones with the same pattern. When you need to spell a word, you use the words you have sorted and spell that word correctly—without even knowing you haven't spelled it before—unless the new word is a word like *playwright* and then you have a 50-50 chance of spelling it correctly. In 1985, Ed Henderson, who spent his entire career studying spelling and who created the idea that children go through various stages in learning to spell, wrote:

> *Those who set out to remember every letter of every word will never make it. Those who try to spell by sound alone will be defeated. Those who learn how to "walk through" words with sensible expectations, noting sound, pattern and meaning relationships will know what to remember, and they will learn to spell English.* (p. 67)

Most English words follow predictable patterns. However, English also contains some completely illogical words that don't follow the patterns. You won't find *they* in your list of *a-y* words along with *stay, may, play, delay,* and *Norway. Want* is not stored along with *hunt, stunt,* and *punt.* Someplace in your brain, you have accumulated a list of words you may have labeled "Words whose spelling makes no sense." In addition to *they* and *want*, this is where you have stored words such as *of, from, people, friend,* and *antique.* The good news is that these illogically spelled words make up a tiny fraction of all the words you can spell. The bad news is that these words (except for *antique*) are among the most common words. It is hard to write a sentence that doesn't contain *have, they, from, are,* or *of.*

Learning to spell in English is a tricky business. On the one hand, you have to start noticing the patterns most words share and using these patterns to spell words because there are just too many words to try to learn them all separately. On the other hand, you have to memorize the ones that don't follow the patterns because they occur so frequently that you can't write without them. If you spell them logically—thay, hav, frum, ar, uv—they will be incorrect and more problematic, because you spell them in the logical but wrong way so often, your brain will assume you are spelling them correctly and these misspellings will become automatic.

In addition to sorting things into patterns, your brain has another very important function. When you do something over and over the same way, your brain puts that action into its "automatic" compartment. This automatic function of your brain is essential to learning because it allows you to do several things at a time as long as all but one of them is automatic. Remember when you were first learning to drive and nothing was automatic? Your brain had to focus on every action:

> "Now, I'm going to turn right. I need to put my right signal on. I am stopping. The light has changed to green. I can give it a little gas and go. I have to watch to make sure no one turns in front of me. Oh, no. It's raining! How do I make the wipers come on? And I need my lights on. Where is that light switch?"

Driving—or any other complex action—is difficult at first because you have to perform many different actions simultaneously and none of them is automatic. (Those of you who, like me, learned to drive with a stick shift and a clutch can multiply the number of simultaneous actions needed!) The more you drive, the more things become automatic—that is, you do them without any conscious thought about doing them.

The fact that your brain makes things automatic after you have done them a certain number of times is essential because you can simultaneously do many automatic things—but only one thing that requires your attention. BUT—your brain does not know the difference between correct and incorrect actions. If you spell words such as *what, come,* and *were* in the logical but wrong way—*wut, cum, wer*—your brain will make these spellings automatic and, as we all know, bad habits are very resistant to change.

If you are a good speller, your brain has at least two word closets. In one relatively small closet are the illogical words you have memorized and now spell automatically because you have spelled them so many times before. Occasionally—but not too often—you encounter a new word such as *plaid*. You figure out this word and immediately decide that *plaid* is not spelled like any of your other rhyming words—*had, glad, bad,* and *nomad*. So, *plaid* gets added to your illogical closet.

In another huge walk-in closet are all other words you can spell—sorted according to patterns. You frequently add words to this closet—perhaps you added *bloggers* to the section where you have your consonant-doubled when adding *er* words. *Blogaholics* may not hang next to *alcoholics* and *chocoholics*. *Blogophobic* hangs alongside your other family members—*claustrophobic, agoraphobic,* and *hydrophobic*. You access the words in your pattern closet regularly, add to them, and use them to figure out the spelling of other words.

I began this book by asking you to evaluate your own spelling skills and think about how you became a good speller. This book, however, is not about you and your spelling but rather about the spelling of your students. Think about your good spellers. Do they make very few spelling errors even when spelling words they haven't studied? Think about your terrible spellers. Do they spell words just the way they sound? Can you read everything they write and do you wonder where to begin to help them learn to spell?

The Scott–Thay Mystery

Many years ago, I taught fourth grade in Terre Haute, Indiana. The smartest—and smallest—boy in my classroom was named Scott. Scott knew everything and was good at everything including spelling—with one exception. He always spelled *they,* t-h-a-y. This was quite a puzzle to me. He could spell *ridiculous, aquarium,* and *desert,* why could he not spell *they?*

They being such a common word, almost every paper Scott wrote contained several *thay*'s. Knowing that future teachers would incorrectly judge his abilities when they saw this common word misspelled, I returned his papers to him with the *thay*'s circled for him to correct. He sighed as he quickly changed the *a*'s to *e*'s and turned the paper back in. By the end of the year, he was spelling *they* correctly but I was still befuddled about why he could not spell *they* correctly when he was otherwise a very good speller.

The next year I went to graduate school at the University of Georgia and as I studied how children learn to decode and spell, I think I solved the mystery. Scott was very bright and he was probably writing long before he had any formal spelling instruction. He was probably also reading before he came to school and had been read a lot of books containing rhyming words. From books like *Hop on Pop* and *One Fish, Two Fish, Red Fish, Blue Fish,* he probably inferred the spelling pattern principle and started storing words in his orthographic store according to pattern.

hop	fish	car	bump	book	old	day
pop	dish	far	hump	cook	bold	say
stop	wish	star	Wump	look	cold	play
plop	swish	jar	Gump	shook	gold	stay

When he was writing and wanted to spell a word, he would use these rhyming words stored in patterns to help him spell and thus could correctly spell words he had never read, such as *flop, squish, bar, stump, hook, fold,* and *stray*. This ability to notice patterns and use them to spell words was what made Scott such an incredibly good speller. It was also why he spelled *they* in the logical—but wrong—way: *thay*. Because *they* is such a common word, he probably wrote *thay* many times and his brain made it automatic. Scott was responsible for my determination to teach young writers the spelling of illogical words early before they become automatic at spelling them logically—but incorrectly!

Spelling matters because students who are not good spellers are rarely good writers. They write as little as possible ("How many sentences do I have to write?") and often they write what they can spell rather than what they want to tell. I have always worried about helping children become fluent, automatic spellers to remove this roadblock to writing for them but currently I find even more reason to worry. Our students today are growing up with texting and Twitter. When you have to type each character on a small phone pad and when your tweet is limited to 140 characters, you often shorten words and use symbols for common words. (*"What r u doing 2nite?"*) Texting and Twitter encourage exactly the kind of spelling behaviors we need to squelch.

Spelling also matters because knowing how a word is spelled has been linked to learning the meaning of that word. In 2008, Rosenthal and Ehri published a clever study in which they investigated if and how knowing the spelling of a word facilitated children's learning of the meaning of that word. They did the study with second- and fifth-graders. The second-graders were shown pictures of objects whose names they were not apt to know. The pictures included a keg, lad, pap, nib, gam, and other very low-frequency nouns. The fifth-graders were shown pictures of objects such as wimple, tandem, laburnum, proboscis, hicatee, and other two- and three-syllable words whose meaning was not apt to be known to fifth-graders (nor to many adults, myself included!). The procedures for teaching the words were the same for the two groups of children at each grade level. They were shown a picture of each object and the name of the object was pronounced. The difference between the groups was that for one group (at each grade level), each picture was accompanied by its printed word. The other group of students saw the pictures without the words. When the students were tested on the meanings of the words, the students in the groups that had seen the spellings recalled more word meanings than the students in the groups that had only seen the pictures without the printed word. This study supports the idea that in learning new word meanings, it helps to have the spelling of the word to link with its meaning and pronunciation.

Finally, spelling matters because of its relationship to reading. Researchers have long found that children's ability to spell is strongly related to their ability to identify words (Berninger, Abbot, Abbot, Graham, & Richards, 2002; Ehri, 1997). Children who are taught to use letter-sound and letter-cluster-sound relationships in their spelling instruction are developing phonemic awareness (Treiman, 1998) and decode words better while reading (Graham, Harris, & Chorzempa, 2002). In two recent studies, learning to spell words with targeted orthographic patterns also improved second- and third-graders' reading of new words containing those same patterns (Conrad, 2008; Shahar-Yames & Share, 2008).

Not only does spelling instruction transfer to improved decoding ability but learning to spell words also helps students learn to recognize them (Conrad, 2008). This effect is a long-term one; adult readers who are poor spellers rely more on context when accessing words and their meanings than good spellers do (Andrews & Bond, 2009).

The purpose of this book is to provide you with a practical spelling program that will enable all your students to become good spellers. If you follow the activities and sequence outlined, your students will learn to spell the illogical words while simultaneously learning how to sort words into spelling patterns and use those sorted words to spell other words.

Chapter 3 details a year's worth of instruction aimed at teaching children how to spell the words they most frequently encounter as they read and write. In addition, the chapter includes 100 key words for all the common beginning consonants, blends, and digraphs and the most common rhyming patterns. The lessons in this chapter will also teach your students how to spell words that end in *s, ed,* and *ing* and that people's names begin with capital letters. The key words and activities in Chapter 3 are appropriate for first-graders and for older children who struggle with literacy or who are just learning to read in English.

In Chapter 4, students learn to spell another 100 key words, which include the remaining high-frequency words and rhyming patterns. They also learn to spell the most common contractions and homophones, the spelling changes that are needed when endings are added to words, and that place names, holidays, and days of the week begin with capital letters. The key words and activities in Chapter 4 are appropriate for students reading at second- and early third-grade levels, including older students whose literacy skills are not at grade level.

Once they have become automatic at spelling the most common words and using the common spelling patterns, students are ready to develop more sophisticated spelling skills. Chapter 5 contains 100 key words and activities that will help your students develop a visual checking sense to determine which of two possible spelling patterns looks right. They also learn spellings and meanings for common homophones and compound words and that the names of months begin with a capital letter. Activities and key words in Chapter 5 are most appropriate for students of any age who read at the fourth-grade level.

Chapter 6 focuses exclusively on polysyllabic words and the complex morphological system in which prefixes and suffixes are added to root words. Students will learn to spell 100 multisyllabic key words and how these key words can unlock the meaning, pronunciation, and spelling of hundreds of other words. Chapter 6's key words and activities are appropriate for students in the upper elementary and middle grades whose reading level is at least fifth grade. Many high school students who struggle with reading or are becoming fluent in English could also benefit from a "crash course" in multisyllabic words based on the activities in this chapter.

All activities in this book are based on the development of a classroom word wall (Cunningham, 2008). The word wall is built gradually—adding 5 words each week—until you have 100 magical words. I call these words "magical words" because, except for the essential illogical words, the words represent a common spelling pattern. When your students learn how to use the patterns in these words, the number of words they can spell grows—like magic. Which words will create the most magic in your classroom depends on the age of the children you teach and their current spelling abilities. Each chapter includes a list of 100 words and assessments to determine if your students need those words and patterns. Chapter 2 will describe how to make your classroom word wall the foundation of your spelling program.

Chapter 2

Building and Using a Classroom Word Wall

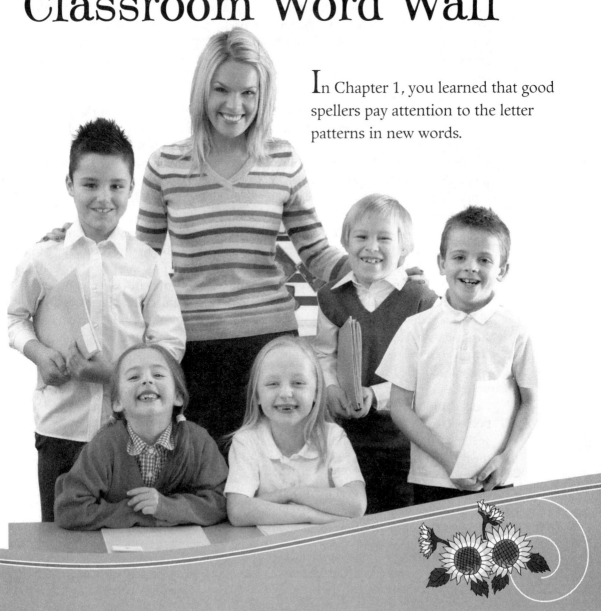

In Chapter 1, you learned that good spellers pay attention to the letter patterns in new words.

In fact, you read about storing words with other words with similar patterns in your brain's orthographic word store. When you encounter new words in your reading, you place them in your brain with other words that have the same pattern. When you are trying to spell a new word, you use the patterns from other words that sound like the new word. To be a good speller, you have to have some words you can spell automatically and these words need to be sorted in your brain according to pattern.

Some students are not good spellers because there are very few words they can spell automatically. A child who spells words by putting down just the letters he or she hears might write a sentence like this:

I lik to pla bol.

This child does not know how to spell the common words *like, play,* and *ball* and thus cannot use the patterns from these words to spell less common words such as *stray, bike,* and *mall*.

Other children can spell some common words but don't use these words to spell other words. Their writing might look like this:

I like to play with Mike. I let Mike ride my bik.

These children can spell *like* and *Mike* but don't use this pattern to spell the word *bike*. They may have lots of words they can spell in their brains but these words might not be sorted according to pattern. I suspect that some children's orthographic word stores look like the insides of their desks: "It's all in there somewhere but it takes a long time to find anything."

The classroom word wall is a concrete external word store that you can use to help all your students put words in their brains' internal word stores. The activities you lead them to do with these words help them to sort the words externally. Your ultimate goal for your students is that they begin placing new words they read in their brains along with other words with similar letter patterns.

Which Words Deserve a Spot on Your Wall?

Word wall words are the most important words for your students to learn. You want every student to learn to quickly and automatically—without thinking—be able to spell **ALL** the words. Furthermore, you want your students to use the words with common patterns to spell other words. To make sure that every student learns them, you have to limit the number of words and provide lots of varied practice with those words. Most teachers find that 100 to 120 words is the maximum number of words they can add. If you add these words gradually—no more than 5 each week—and provide daily practice with these words, **ALL** your students should be able to achieve the goal of automatic spelling of these words. Making wise decisions about which words to include on your wall is critical. Each of the next four chapters includes a list of 100 critical words. These words were carefully chosen to include the most frequently occurring words and patterns. The first 100 words are words that will be most useful to first-graders and should form the basis of your list if you teach first grade. The first 100 words contains the most common words, the most common rhyming patterns, and an example for all the common consonants, digraphs, and blends. For words with helpful rhyming patterns, these patterns are highlighted. In addition to these words and patterns, your students will also learn to spell words with *s, ed,* and *ing* endings without spelling changes and to capitalize the first letter of people's names.

100 Key Words to Teach the Most Common Words and Patterns				
a	all	am	and	are
at	be	best	big	black
boy	bright	but	can	children
clown	coat	comes	crashing	did
do	drink	each	eat	flag
flew	for	friend	from	girl
go	good	grow	had	has
have	he	her	here	his
how	I	If	in	is
it	jump	kind	like	little
look	made	make	me	my
not	of	old	on	out
pet	play	price	quick	ride
run	said	saw	see	she
skate	sleep	smart	snap	so
some	spell	stop	swim	talk
the	there	they	thing	this
to	train	up	very	wanted
was	we	went	what	when
will	with	you	your	zoos

Unfortunately, many older children cannot correctly spell the words in this list or can spell the words but not other words with the same rhyming pattern. If you teach older children, you can use the diagnostic assessments in each chapter to determine which of the words from the first 100 you need to begin your word wall with before moving to the more advanced lists.

The second group of 100 words includes other common words and patterns, common contractions and homophones, and spelling changes required when endings are added. In addition, by adding your name, the name of your city or town, your school, two names of days of the week, and a holiday such as Thanksgiving, your students will learn that names of specific places, days, and holidays begin with capital letters. If you teach second grade and your students know almost all the words and patterns from the first 100, you can add the ones they need from that list and then finish your word wall with the words from the second 100. If you teach older students, you need to decide which words your students need from the second 100. Chapter 4 contains some diagnostic assessments you can use to determine this.

100 Key Words for Common Words, Patterns, Contractions, and Homophones				
about	after	again	almost	also
always	animal	aren't	around	because
bedroom	before	birthday	brother	build
busy	campfire	can't	catches	city
could	cousin	does	don't	*families*
family	favorite	*flies*	football	funny
getting	*glasses*	*goes*	great	holiday
homework	hundred	I'll	I'm	into
it's	know	laugh	many	**Monday**
myself	no	off	once	outside
over	people	place	pretty	really
right	**Saturday**	school	shouldn't	sister
skateboard	spoke	sport	stopped	street
summer	surprise	*swimming*	teacher	thank
Thanksgiving	their	there	they're	to

tomorrow	too	*tried*	two	under
until	*used*	wasn't	we're	wear
weekend	were	what's	where	who
why	winter	*wishes*	without	write
writing	**teacher name**	**school name**	**street name**	**city/town name**

The third group of 100 words includes "spelling demons," spelling changes needed when adding common endings, and more common homophones. In addition, by adding the names of your state and country and the names of some months, your students will learn that particular places and months are spelled with capital letters. The focus of Chapter 5 is on helping students develop a visual checking sense. Words that rhyme but have different spelling patterns, such as *meal* and *wheel,* are used in *What Looks Right?* lessons to help your students develop that sense. If you teach third or fourth grade and your students know almost all the words and patterns from the first and second 100, you can add the ones they need from these lists and then finish your word wall with the words from the third 100. If you teach older students, you need to decide if your students have a visual checking sense. Chapter 5 contains a diagnostic assessment you can use to determine this.

100 Key Words Including Spelling Demons and Homphones				
accept	afraid	although	**America**	another
answer	anyone	bait	bare	bear
bed	believe	biggest	brake	bread
break	buy	by	caught	chair
cheer	close	clothes	code	country
crane	**December**	during	eight	either
enough	everybody	except	exciting	**February**
finally	float	grade	green	*happier*
hidden	hole	hour	however	interesting
June	knew	listen	loan	machine
meal	mean	million	minute	month
neighbor	new	often	one	our

own	peace	phone	picture	piece
probably	restaurant	snowed	something	son
soon	special	state	sun	terrible
thought	thousand	threw	through	together
tonight	trail	train	trouble	true
United States	unload	unusual	vacation	vote
weather	whale	wheel	whether	white
whole	*winner*	won	year	**your state name**

In Chapter 6, you will find 100 "big words," which are key words for all the common prefixes and suffixes along with spelling changes. Students who leave elementary school able to spell all 400 words have the words and patterns stored in their brains that will enable them to spell most words they need throughout the remaining school years.

100 Big Key Words				
acceptable	action	adventure	agreement	antibiotics
apartment	artist	beautiful	classify	cloudy
command	competition	complete	composition	conclude
confidence	confident	continue	coolest	creative
dangerous	defective	defend	defense	defensive
delicious	design	destroy	destruction	different
direction	disappear	discovery	dishonest	effective
electricity	encourage	enormous	entertain	equal
excitement	explode	exploration	explosion	explosive
exports	flexible	forgotten	governor	happiness
hopeless	hotter	identification	immigrant	important
impossible	impression	impressive	incorrect	indent
independent	information	inspector	interesting	intersection
inventor	invisible	magical	migrate	misunderstood

mountainous	musician	mystery	nation	nonviolent
offender	offense	overweight	performance	politics
prediction	preview	produce	production	promotion
protective	rebuild	recall	remember	sensitive
signature	strengthen	sunny	swimmer	transfer
unbelievable	underground	unhappily	valuable	weaken

Building Your Word Wall

You are probably now convinced that there is a core group of words that all your students need to learn to spell so that they can concentrate their thinking power on what they are writing, and the words will be written the way you write them—automatically without conscious thought. Now you must make a tangible commitment to this goal. You have to allocate to your word wall some of your valuable classroom space. If all your students are going to learn these words, the words must be kept on display all year and must be somewhere that your students can see them at all times—particularly when they are writing. In some classrooms, the space above the board at the front of the room will work. In other classrooms, a large bulletin board or chalkboard can be allocated to the word wall. If none of these works in your classroom, you may have to get creative. Perhaps you have a large wall all your students can see. Thanks to the miracle of sticky clips, you can attach things to rough walls that never would have stayed in the days of masking tape. If you have a whole wall of windows, you might cover some of these windows with pull down shades—which you leave down—and attach your words to them. Some classrooms have a large wall of cabinets. Your word wall can stretch across all the cabinets and be visible to your students as long as the cabinets are closed. In classrooms, there is never enough space to do everything you would like to do. If your word wall is going to be the foundation of your spelling program and if you want all your students to learn to spell the critical words, you have to give your word wall some of your prime real estate.

Once you have chosen a place, you will want to display the words under the letter they begin with so that students can quickly find a word. Think ahead to the words you want when the word wall is complete and spread out your letters accordingly. You are not going to have many words that begin with *J, K,* or *L,* but you are probably going to have a bunch of words that begin with *S, T,* and *W.* The diagram of the word wall without any words added shows how one teacher spread out the letters to accommodate the words he planned to add.

Aa   Bb   Cc   Dd   Ee   Ff   Gg

Hh   Ii   Jj   Kk   Ll   Mm   Nn   Oo   Pp   Qq

Rr   Ss   Tt   Uu   Vv

Ww   Xx   Yy   Zz

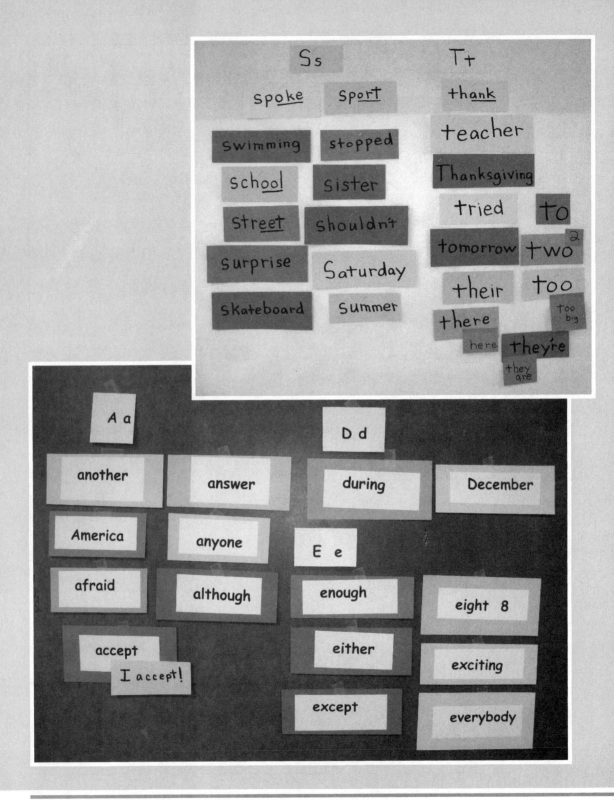

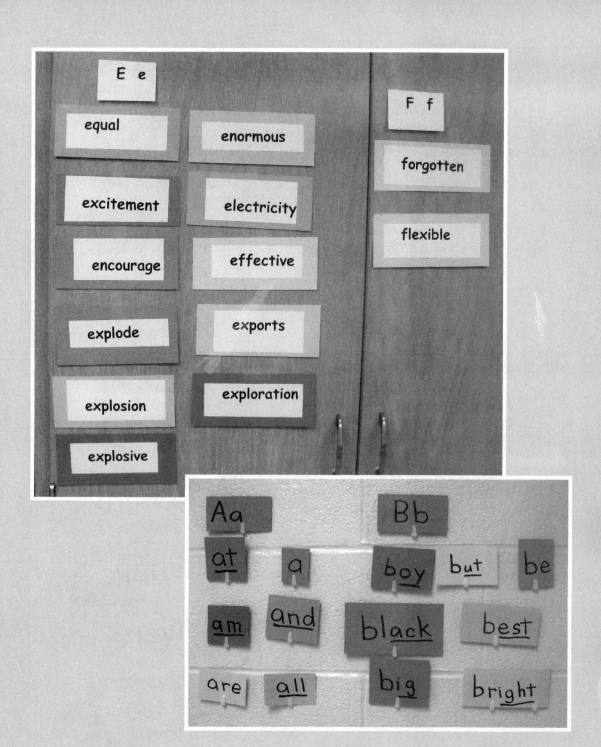

Now think about what you are going to write the words on. The words have to be big enough so that they can be seen from anywhere in the room. You will want to use different colors to make your word wall more appealing and to help your students distinguish between the confusable words such as *want, went, what; that, they, them; for, from;* and *of, off.* When adding a word that would be easily confused with another word, use a different color for the new word. A pack of multicolor index paper will give you several colors to choose from and should accommodate all your words. Many teachers combine their daily word wall practice with handwriting practice and cut around the shape of the words to help students concretely see the tall letters and those that go below the line. Cutting around the configuration is also a helpful cue to those confusable words. Children who are looking for *where* tend to distinguish it from *were* by its "*h* sticking up." Write the words with a black thick marker and cut around the word to show the shape and the size.

If you are a teacher who does everything on your computer, you can type the words with a large bold font, print them out on white paper and then back the word with different colors.

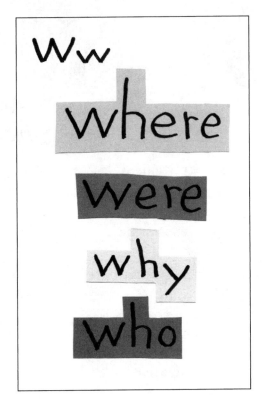

The Daily Word Wall Practice

After you have created a place front and center for your word wall and created the word cards so that they are big and bold and easily distinguished from one another, you need to give your word wall 10 to 12 minutes of your precious classroom time. If all your students are going to learn all the words, they will need daily practice with the words, and this practice cannot be the traditional practice we give to spelling words. Your children who struggle with spelling won't learn these words (and they never have!) by writing the words five times, putting them in alphabetical order, writing a definition, or writing each word in a sentence. The problem with all these traditional practice activities is that they are highly visual and not very engaging. To practice the words, get your students out of their seats and lead them to "cheer" the words. (Pom poms are optional!) The children enjoy this cheering. More importantly, in cheering the words, they are using their auditory learning channel. After the cheering, have your students sit down and, following your model, write the words. In writing the words, they are using their kinesthetic—or muscular—learning channel. Writing the words in this teacher-directed way is different from the mindless way most children write their spelling words five times each. Do you remember what you did when you were a kid? To get the word *they* written five times, did you write five *t*'s first, then add five *h*'s, five *e*'s, and five *y*'s ? This is the most efficient way to accomplish this mind-numbing task but it doesn't help solidify the order of the letters in the word.

t	th	the	they
t	th	the	they
t	th	the	they
t	th	the	they
t	th	the	they

Each day, have your students stand up and lead them in cheering five words—three times for each word. With the wiggles out, sit them back down and model how to write the five words. This is when many teachers practice handwriting each day. If you want to kill two birds with one stone, have your students write the five words on handwriting paper and model for them the correct handwriting. When the five words are written, fence in each of your words so they can see the shape of the word when the tall and below the line letters are correctly placed. Have them check their word by fencing it in and seeing if "their fence matches your fence."

Add the words gradually, no more than five words each week. On the day you add new words, these new words are the words you lead your students to cheer for and model handwriting for. Cheer and write these same five new words on the second day. During the rest of the week, however, choose any five words from the wall for practice. Focus on the more difficult words, calling them out regularly until all students can spell them without looking. Every four or five weeks, take a week or two off from adding words and review by using some of the review games and activities described in each chapter.

Many teachers like to begin their word walls with the names of their students. Explain to the children that the word wall space is reserved for the most important words—words everyone needs to learn to spell. Since they are the most important people in your classroom, their names will be the first words added to the wall. Add one or two each day. Lead your students to cheer for and write their names and they will establish a positive attitude toward the wall, which should carry over when you begin adding the boring but essential key words.

"If It's on the Word Wall, It HAS to Be Spelled Correctly"

Choosing the words carefully, displaying them in a visually appealing way, and providing 10 to 12 minutes of daily practice with the words will go a long way toward helping all your students learn these critical key words. But, if some of your students have already learned an incorrect spelling—t-h-a-y for *they*, g-r-i-l for *girl*, t-o for all the homophones *two, to,* and *too*—they are apt to continue misspelling these in their writing in spite of the word wall practice you provide. Remember from Chapter 1 that once your brain has performed some actions a number of times, that action becomes automatic. Automatic is good when what you have done several times was done correctly. Unfortunately, when you practice it wrong many times, it becomes automatically wrong! Remember Scott, my brilliant fourth-grader who could spell all kinds of sophisticated words but spelled *they* t-h-a-y? Scott had

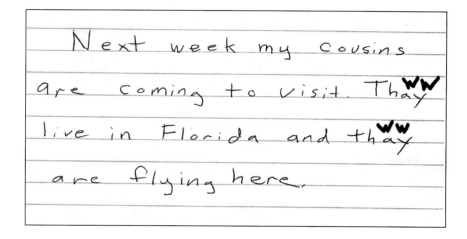

Next week my cousins
are coming to visit. Th**ay**
live in Florida and th**ay**
are flying here.

written it that way so many times that when he was writing, he spelled it that way automatically—without any conscious thought.

Once you have a word on your word wall, require that all your students spell it correctly in everything they write. When you see it spelled incorrectly, simply write WW (word wall) over it and require the student to correct it. Before too long, when that student is writing and begins to spell a word in the old, automatic but incorrect way, this child's brain will think "WW" and he or she will glance at the word wall and correct it. Old habits are hard to break but they can be broken and new habits can be learned if you are consistent and persistent.

Personal Word Walls

In addition to your classroom word wall, you may want to create personal word walls for your students whose spelling skills lag way behind those of the other students. Perhaps you have only one or two students who spell *they* t-h-a-y or just a few students who can't spell basic rhyming pattern words such as *like* and *car*. For those students, you can create personal word walls containing just those words they need to learn. A file folder is the perfect vehicle for a personal word wall. Use both inside pages and divide the space alphabetically, leaving less space for letters such as *j, k,* and *l* and more space for *s, t,* and *w*. Add one or two words each week to the personal word walls of your lagging spellers, choosing words based on the assessments included in each chapter or common words or patterns you notice they are misspelling in their writing. Make sure they have their personal word walls out whenever they write and remind them to use their personal word walls in addition to the classroom word wall to spell words correctly.

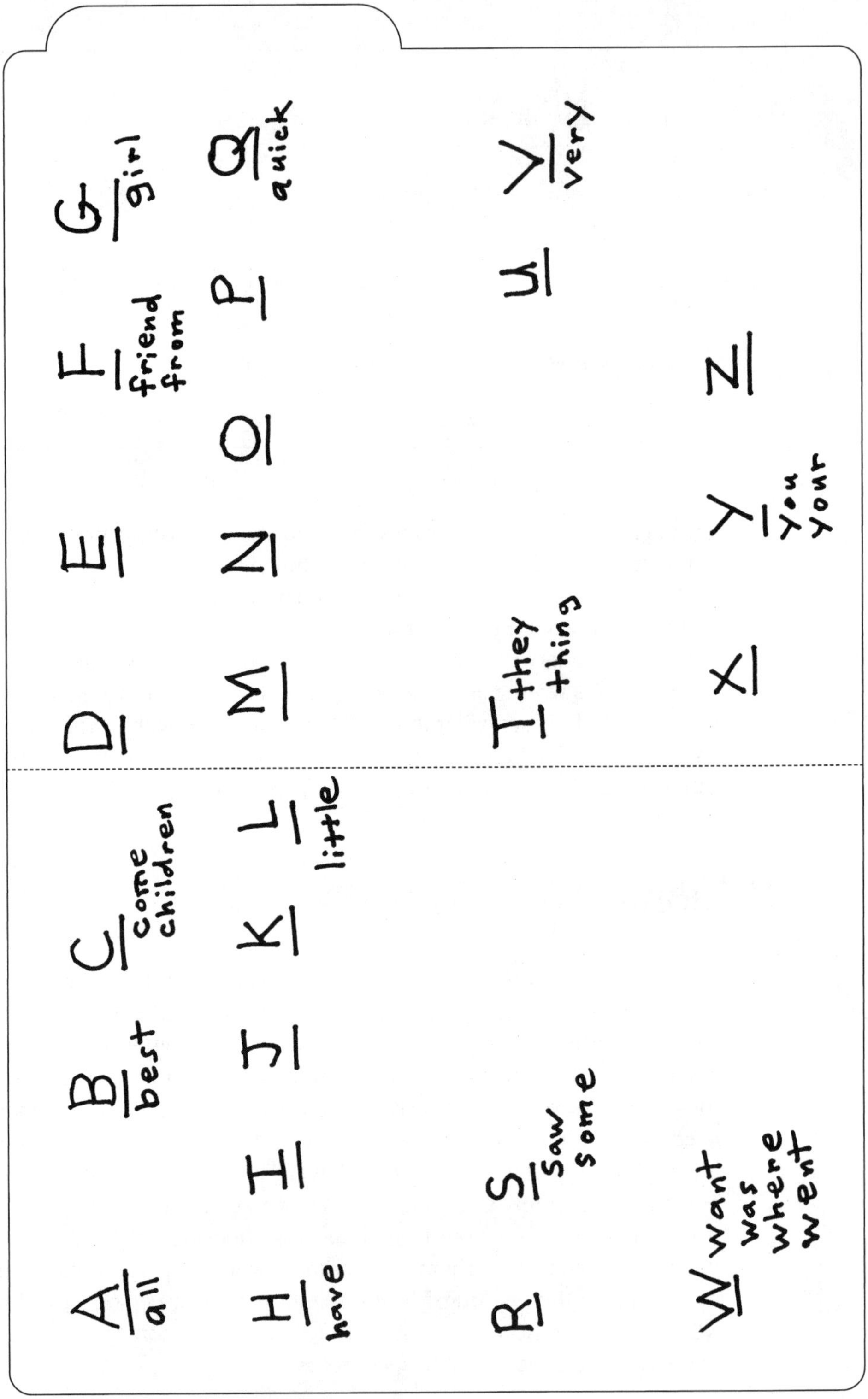

A — all
B — best
C — come, children
D
E
F — friend, from
G — girl

H — have
I
J
K
L — little
M
N
O
P
Q — quick

R — saw, some
S
T — they, thing
U
V — very

W — want, was, where, went
X
Y — you, your
Z

Getting the Most Out of Your Word Wall

Perhaps you have used a word wall in years past and haven't seen the results from it you expected. In some classrooms, word walls are little more than decorations. Words on these decorative walls may not be the words most needed by your class of students. Once put on the wall, these words were likely not given daily attention and were often ignored by the students. To make your word wall the centerpiece of your spelling instruction, you need to:

- Choose the words most needed by your students.
- Add words gradually, no more than five each week.
- Display the words in bright colors in a space everyone can see.
- Provide daily auditory and kinesthetic practice with the words through cheering and writing.
- Review words with activities and games that engage your students.
- Create personal word walls for students whose spelling skills lag way behind those of most of the other students.

The word wall that will teach all your students to spell and organize words in their brains must be an active, growing, integral part of your classroom.

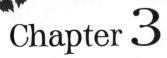

Chapter 3

Teaching the 100 Most Common Words and Patterns

The major reason to teach children to spell is to enable them to write. Research has shown that handwriting and spelling are highly predictive of writing fluency.

Children who can form the letters easily and spell most of the words correctly write faster and with greater ease (Graham, Berninger, Abbott, Abbott, & Whitaker, 1997). There is also evidence that teaching spelling has a positive effect on writing fluency (Berninger, Vaughan, Abbott, Brooks, Abbott, Reid, et al. (1998). Beringer, Abbot, Abbot, Graham, and Richards (2002) provided 48 20-minute spelling mini-lessons to second-graders experiencing difficulty learning to spell. After 16 hours of spelling instruction, these second-graders showed significant improvement on standardized spelling, decoding, and writing fluency measures.

As young children begin to write, they often represent words with the letter sounds they hear. *Bike* is spelled b-i-k. *Look* is spelled l-o-k. This invented or phonic spelling is a totally appropriate way for young children to begin writing, and there is research that demonstrates that first-graders encouraged to use this invented spelling write more and actually learn more phonics (Clarke, 1988). As children develop some ability to read and write, however, they need to learn the correct spelling for the words they write most often. This is easy for common words such as *at, be,* and *go,* where putting down letters for the sounds you hear results in the correct spelling, but how will your beginning writers spell *come, they,* and *was?* If they are spelling these words the way they sound, these words will probably be spelled c-u-m, t-h-a-y, and w-u-z. And because these words occur very frequently, the children will spell them c-u-m, t-h-a-y, and w-u-z many times. When you do something over and over, your brain makes that automatic. Before long, when your students are writing and thinking about what they want to say, common words such as *come, they,* and *was* will be spelled in the logical—but incorrect—way.

Beginning writers of any age need to learn to spell the most frequent words. The high-frequency words taught in these lessons were selected based on two major studies of word frequency (Carroll, Davies, & Richman, 1971; Zeno, Ivens, Millard, & Duvvuri, 1995). The most frequent words are included in this chapter. The remainder of the most frequent words are included in Chapter 4.

In addition to learning to spell the most frequent words, children need to move from one-letter–one-sound spelling to a spelling pattern strategy. Most one-syllable English words are composed of two patterns. The first pattern is the beginning letters—everything up to the vowel—which teachers call consonants, blends, and digraphs, and linguists call onsets. The second part—which teachers call the rhyming pattern and linguists call a rime—begins at the vowel and goes to the end of the word. The two patterns in the word *black* are b-l and a-c-k. In *bright,* they are b-r and i-g-h-t. In *thing,* they are t-h and i-n-g. Although some of these patterns seem illogical, they are almost totally consistent across other words. If words sound like *black, bright,* or *thing* at the beginning, the onset is almost surely spelled b-l, b-r, and t-h. Most words that rhyme with *black, bright,* and *thing*—*crack, shack; light, night; sting, fling*—share the same rime. When your students know the beginning letter patterns and the most common rhyming patterns, they can spell hundreds of words. Research has shown that primary-grade children can spell new words based on patterns if they can spell other words that share that same pattern (Bosse, Valdois, & Tainturier, 2003). The 100 words in this chapter contain a key word for all the common beginning letter patterns and for the most common rhyming patterns (Wylie & Durrell, 1970).

A final spelling pattern young children need to learn is how to spell words with common endings. This chapter includes key words for adding *s* (*comes; zoos*), *ed* (*wanted*), and *ing* (*crashing*). The second set of 100 words (in Chapter 4) contains key words to teach students how to spell words with endings that require spelling changes.

The remainder of this chapter contains lists, diagnostic paragraphs, and activities for teaching the 100 most important words all elementary students need to be able to spell. The 100 words are divided into 4 sets of 25 each. Each set contains some common, illogically spelled high-frequency words (*want, have, said*) and other words that are key words for beginning sounds and rhyming patterns (*look, quick, crash*).

If you teach first grade, having all your students learn to spell these 100 words should be your goal. If you teach older students, paragraphs are included that you can dictate to your students to determine which words your students need. It is very important to use the paragraph dictation rather than a traditional spelling test to make this determination. Remember from Chapter 1 that a human brain can do many automatic things and only one non-automatic thing at a time. If you simply dictate the words in spelling test form, many students will spell words correctly that they will then spell incorrectly when they are writing. When taking a spelling test, your students can allocate all their attention to spelling the words. If they are trying to spell *they,* for example, they might start to write t-h-a-y but then notice that it doesn't look right and change the spelling. Later, when your students are writing, their non-automatic attention is being used to think about what they are writing and words that are not automatic will be spelled in a logical—but incorrect—way.

The First 25 Words

Here are the words we begin our spelling instruction with:

a	and	at	big	boy	can	do
eat	for	girl	go	he	I	is
in	jump	like	look	me	not	pet
run	see	the	to			

This first 25 words list contains some of the most common words in the English language. It is nearly impossible to write a sentence and not use the word *a, I, and, the, is, in,* or *to.* In addition, there is a clear example for the most common consonants: *b, c, d, f, g, h, j, l, m, n, p, r, s,* and *t* and for common rhyming patterns: *an, and, at, eat, ee, et, ig, ike, in, ook, ot, oy, ump,* and *un.* The goal for this list is that your students should be able to spell all 25 words and rhyming words that begin with the common consonants. If you teach first grade, you will want to begin your word wall with these 25 words, adding them gradually each week.

Do Your Older Students Need Any of These First 25 Words?

If you teach older children, you need to decide which, if any, of these words to include. Most second-graders and older children can spell all 25 of these words, know the sounds for the common single consonants, and can spell rhyming words that begin with the common single consonants. To determine if your students need any of these words on the wall, dictate the following paragraph to them and have them write it without any help from you.

> <u>Roy</u> **is** a <u>fun</u> **pet. He is** a <u>fat</u> <u>pig</u>. **The girl and boy** <u>took</u> <u>Roy</u> **to run in the** <u>sand</u> <u>lot.</u>

Before dictating the paragraph to your students, be sure they are seated where they can't see each other's papers and tell them you want to see what writing skills they need to work on and they should just do the best they can. Do not tell them you are assessing their spelling. If they ask you how to spell a word, simply tell them to "do the best you can." Keep a reasonable pace in your dictation—giving the students enough time to get the words down but not enough to labor over the spelling of each word. Remember, you are trying to get a snapshot of their spelling proficiency while writing so that you can determine which words need to be a part of your word wall and spelling instruction.

Assess their entering spelling levels by considering the three criteria this set of words is intended to teach:

- Look at the spelling of the bold words (**is, a, pet, he, the, girl, and, boy, to, run, in**) to determine if any of these common words are misspelled by any of your students. The bold words are included to help you determine if they can spell the first 25 words.

- Look at the first letter in the underlined words (<u>R</u>oy, <u>f</u>un, <u>f</u>at, <u>p</u>ig, <u>t</u>ook, <u>s</u>and, <u>l</u>ot) to determine if they know the common single consonant sounds (r, f, p, t, s, l).

- Look at the italicized words (*Roy, fun, fat, pig, took, sand, lot*) to determine if they can use common words they know to spell rhyming words with a single consonant.

(continued)

If you determine that some of your students need some of these words, begin your word wall with whichever words they need—adding no more than five words each week and doing the activities described in this chapter to teach the words, the consonant sounds, and how to use rhyming words to spell other words. When you have added the words you need and provided lots of practice with those words, dictate the paragraph to them again. When your students can spell all the words in this paragraph, dictate the paragraph for the next 25 words to determine which of these words they need.

● What if Only a Few of My Students Need These Words?

In every classroom there will be students whose spelling skills lag way behind the skills of the rest of the class. This makes it difficult to determine which words to focus your time and attention on. The most practical solution seems to be to add words to the wall that more than a few of your students need, and to create personal word walls for those students who need to learn to spell words everyone else can already spell. Chapter 2 (pp. 21–22) described how to create a file folder personal word wall for your lagging spellers. Add a few words each week to their personal word wall and make sure they have the file folder visible whenever they write. Include these students in the activities with your class word wall and hold them accountable in their writing for words on the class word wall and on their personal word walls.

● Teaching the First 25 Words and Common Consonant Sounds

These 25 words contain the most common words and a key word for the most common consonants: *b, c, d, f, g, h, j, l, m, n, p, r, s,* and *t.* Your goal in teaching these 25 words is that all your students learn to spell all 25 words and use the words with the highlighted or underlined patterns to spell rhyming words that begin with these common consonants.

a	and	at	big	boy	can	do
eat	for	girl	go	he	I	is
in	jump	like	look	me	not	pet
run	see	the	to			

When you begin adding these words to your word wall, the word wall should already display the names of all your students. Choose five words that, along with the names of your students, can make a sentence, perhaps *a, big, boy, girl,* and *is.* Put these words on your wall and help your students use these words in oral sentences.

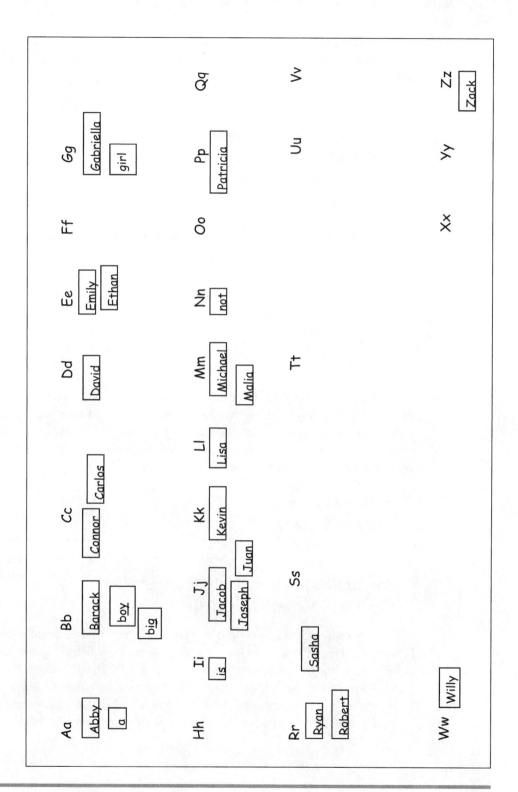

Aa Abby a

Bb Barack boy big

Cc Connor Carlos

Dd David

Ee Emily Ethan

Ff

Gg Gabriella girl

Hh

Ii is

Jj Jacob Joseph Juan

Kk Kevin

Ll Lisa

Mm Michael Malia

Nn not

Oo

Pp Patricia

Qq

Rr Ryan Robert

Ss Sasha

Tt

Uu

Vv

Ww Willy

Xx

Yy

Zz Zack

Get your students out of their seats and lead them to cheer for the five words—three times each word. Have them say the word they are cheering at the beginning and end.

"big b-i-g; b-i-g; b-i-g; big"

"boy b-o-y; b-o-y; b-o-y; boy"

"girl g-i-r-l; g-i-r-l; g-i-r-l; girl"

"is i-s; i-s; i-s; is"

"a a; a; a; a"

Next, have them write the words as you model correct letter formation.

boy

girl

a

big

is

For the next several days, continue to lead your students to cheer for and write these words. Point out to them that the words *boy* and *girl* do not begin with a capital letter because they are not the names of specific boys and girls. When they have written the words in a list for two or three days, dictate some sentences for them to write and model how to use these words in sentences.

Kevin is a big boy.

Emily is a big girl.

Spelling Skills Help Only if the Students Use Them When They Write!

The only reason your students need to learn how to spell words is to enable them to write fluently and well. If they learn to spell words during your spelling practice but do not spell them correctly when writing, your spelling practice is wasted. Provide weekly practice in spelling the word wall words as the children write a few sentences. When they are writing throughout the day, remind them to use the word wall and hold them accountable for spelling word wall words correctly in everything they write.

Use the words that are examples for the common consonants to build that letter-sound connection. If *boy* and *girl* were two of your first words, say some words that begin with *b* or *g* (*go; good; box; bike; book; got; gift; bus; game*) and have your students tell you whether they begin with a *b* like *boy* or a *g* like *girl*.

When all your students can spell the first five words quickly and automatically and when they know the sounds for the common consonants you have taught in your first five words, add five more words. Say some sentences using the new words to make sure your students have these words in their oral vocabulary. Lead your students to cheer the new words—three times each:

"can c-a-n; c-a-n; c-a-n; can"

"jump j-u-m-p; j-u-m-p; j-u-m-p; jump"

"run r-u-n; r-u-n; r-u-n; run"

"and a-n-d; a-n-d; a-n-d; and"

"I capital I; capital I; capital I; I"

Model how to write the new words and have the students write them.

can

run

I

jump

and

Use the key words to teach the common consonant sounds by saying other words that begin with these letters and having your students decide what word wall word they begin like. If you added *jump, can,* and *run,* have the children use these key words to decide what letters begin common words such as *come, rice, camp, jar, cold,* and *rain.*

Focus on these five new words for two days. Then spend three days practicing new and old words. Each day lead your students to cheer for five words but include some of the old words with some new words. Model for your students how to write sentences that include their names and all the words on the wall.

Zack can jump and run.

Abby can jump and run.

I can run.

I can jump.

A boy and a girl can jump and run.

Continue to add five words each week following these procedures for each group of words.

- Use new words in sentences to make sure your students have them in their oral vocabulary.
- For two days, focus only on the new words by leading your students to cheer for and write the new words.
- Use words with common consonants as key words for these sounds and teach your students how to use these key words to figure out the beginning letter for other common words.
- For three days, choose five words to cheer for, including some old words and some of the new words.
- Model sentences for your students to write that include new and old words.
- Provide lots of practice with all the key words so that your students are very comfortable telling what letter words begin with when those words begin with the letters *b, c, d, f, g, h, j, l, m, n, p, r, s,* and *t.*

● Review the First 25 Words

When you have all 25 words on your wall, take a few weeks to consolidate your word wall words and sounds. WORDO is the simplest and most engaging review activity. Make copies of a sheet with nine squares. Have your children choose 9 of the 25 words and write them—one to a square. Meanwhile, make yourself a deck of calling cards by writing the 25 words on index cards—one to a card. When your students have their WORDO sheets ready, shuffle your cards and call out words until someone has covered all the words on their card. The first person to cover the card completely is the winner and should shout, "WORDO." Check to see that all the words they covered were called and they are all spelled correctly on their sheet. If you have time, have the students clear their cards and play another round. Using Cheerios or some other nutritious cereal to cover the words makes for quick clean-up and a nutritious snack!

jump	look	I
pet	boy	and
see	run	do

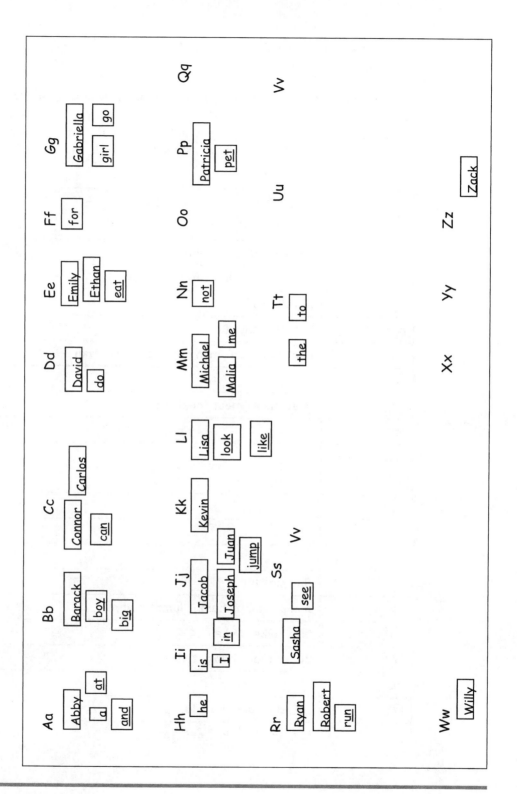

Teaching Your Students to Spell Rhyming Words

When your students can spell the 25 first words and know the sounds for the common consonants, it is time to help them extend their spelling skills to spelling words that rhyme with word wall words and begin with the single consonants. This chart lists the rhyming words your students should be able to spell.

Set 1	b, c, d, f, g, h, j, l, m, n, p, r, s, t
a	
and	band hand land sand
at	bat cat fat hat mat Nat pat Pat rat sat
big	dig fig pig
boy	joy Joy toy Roy
can	ban Dan fan man Nan pan ran tan
do	
eat	beat heat meat neat seat
for	
girl	
go	
he	
I	
is	
in	fin pin tin
jump	bump dump hump lump pump
like	bike hike Mike
look	book cook hook took
me	
not	cot dot got hot lot pot rot
pet	bet get jet let net set

run	bun fun gun sun
see	bee fee
the	
to	

To teach the children to use the words they know to spell other words, use the following lesson format. Give your students a sheet of paper that looks like this. Create the same sheet for you to write on using your board or chart paper.

Choose three of the highlighted words that have a very different rhyming pattern. Write these three words at the top of the column and have your students write them in their columns. Demonstrate for them how to underline or highlight the rhyming pattern in each word. (When you use *at, and, in,* and *eat,* make sure they understand the rhyming pattern is the whole word.)

look	boy	at

Say some words that rhyme with *look, boy,* and *at* and use each word in a sentence. Be sure to include some names that rhyme and to remind students that all specific names, not just their own, begin with a capital letter.

"took   We took our sick dog to the vet."

"Roy   I have a cousin named Roy."

Ask your students to pronounce each word and tell you which word it rhymes with. Then ask them what letter the word begins with. If they need help in deciding the beginning letter, remind them of the key words they have learned for each letter.

b boy big	c can	d do	f for
g girl	h he	j jump	l look
m me	n not	p pet	r run
s see	t to		

Now demonstrate for the students how to spell a new word by writing the first letter and then adding the rhyming pattern. After they write each word, have them underline or highlight (they love highlighters!) the rhyming pattern and notice that they are the same. When the chart is finished, have them notice that the 3 words they know helped them spell 12 more words! Lead them to cheer for the words in each column:

"l-o-o-k: look; b-o-o-k: book; t-o-o-k: took; c-o-o-k: cook; h-o-o-k: hook"

"b-o-y: boy; j-o-y: joy; t-o-y: toy; R-o-y: Roy"

"a-t: at; c-a-t: cat; s-a-t: sat; h-a-t: hat; f-a-t: fat; r-a-t: rat"

look	boy	at
book	joy	cat
took	toy	sat
cook	Roy	hat
hook		fat
		rat

To make sure they understand that you want them to use these rhyming spelling patterns when they are writing, model how to write a sentence that uses a few of the rhyming words and some word wall words. Ask your students to write this sentence or another sentence they think of using word wall words and rhyming words from the chart. Don't worry if the limited vocabulary results in silly sentences. Children like silly!

Roy took the cook to see the fat cat.

Over the next two or three weeks, continue this procedure of having your students use three rhyming words to spell words and then writing one sentence that contains word wall words and rhyming words they have written. For the first lessons, choose rhyming words with quite different sounds.

big	eat	and
pig	seat	sand
wig	beat	land
dig	neat	hand
	meat	band
	heat	

The boy and girl like to dig in the sand.

For later lessons, choose words in which the rhyming sounds are similar.

run	in	can
fun	fin	man
bun	tin	tan
sun	pin	Dan
gun		pan
		Nan

Nan and Dan like to run in the sun.

If your students enjoyed playing WORDO to review the word wall words, you can use this same game to review the rhyming words. Choose three of the word wall words with rhyming patterns. Write all the rhyming words on index cards. Show the index cards to your students and let them choose nine words to write in the squares. Shuffle your index card deck and call out words until someone shouts, "WORDO." Check to be sure all covered words were called and are spelled correctly.

Mike	jet	bike
land	bet	band
sand	hike	net

The Second 25 Words

When all your students can spell the first 25 word wall words and most of your children can spell most of the rhyming words with common single consonants, you are ready to begin working with the second set:

all	be	best	children	comes	good	have
here	it	kind	make	out	play	quick
ride	said	she	they	up	very	went
what	will	you	zoos			

This second set of 25 words contains some very common words that many students spell in the logical but wrong way (*come, have, here, said, they, very,* and *what*). In addition, there is a clear example for the less common consonants *k, v, w, y,* and *z,* and for the digraphs *ch, sh, th, wh,* and *qu.* There are also examples for the common spelling patterns *ake, all, am, ay, ent, est, ide, ill, ind, it, out,* and *up.* While teaching this set of words, you will also teach the children to spell words with the *s* ending. *Comes* and *zoos* are examples of *s*-ending words. The goal for this list is that your students should be able to spell all 25 words and rhyming words that begin single consonants and *sh, ch, th, wh,* and *qu.* If you teach first grade, you will want to continue your word wall with these 25 words.

If You Teach Older Children

If you teach older children, you need to decide which, if any, of these words to include. Many second-graders and older children misspell the common illogical words *come, have, here, said, they, very,* and *what*. Other children can spell common words— *best*—but not rhyming words such as *rest* or *chest*. To determine if your students need any of these words on the wall, dictate the following paragraph to them and have them write it without any help from you.

> **All** the **children went** to the *lake* to **play**. A *quake* *shook* the land. *Thump*, the *tide* *hit* the *tent*s. **They** got *wet*. *Nick* **said**, "**It will be best** to *take* the *van* and go."

Seat your students so that they cannot see what anyone else is writing. Tell them that you want to assess their writing and they should do the best they can. Keep a reasonable pace that does not allow them to labor over the spelling of words. Assess their spelling needs by considering the three criteria this set of words is intended to teach.

- Look at the spelling of the bold words (**all, children, went, play, they, said, it, will, be, best**.) to determine if any of these common words are misspelled by any of your students.
- Look at the first letter in the underlined words (qu, sh, th, w, v) to determine if they know the digraph and less common consonant sounds.
- Look at the italicized words (*lake, quake, shook, thump, tide, hit, tents, wet, Nick, take, van*) to determine if they can use common words they know to spell rhyming words with consonants and digraphs.

If you determine that your students need some of these words, add whichever words they need—to your wall, adding no more than five words each week. When you have added the words they need and provided lots of practice with those words and rhyming words, dictate the paragraph to them again. If only a few children need these words, add the word gradually to their personal word walls.

● Teaching the Second 25 Words

The second set of 25 words contains more high-frequency words and an example for the less common consonants and digraphs. The highlighted words contain a rhyming pattern your students can use to spell many other words. Another goal to accomplish while you teach these words is to teach your students to spell words with the *s* ending.

all	be	best	children	comes	good	have
here	it	kind	make	out	play	quick
ride	said	she	they	up	very	went
what	will	you	zoos			

Use the procedures described in the previous section to teach your students to spell the 25 words, the sounds for *v, w, z, ch, sh, th, wh,* and *qu,* and how to spell words that rhyme with the word wall words.

- Add words to the wall gradually, no more than five each week.

- On the day you add new words and the following day, lead your students to cheer three times for each new word and model the writing of each word.

- When you add the key words for k (*kind*), v (*van*), w (*will, went*), y (*you*), z (*zoos*), ch (*children*), sh (*she*), th (*they*), wh (*what*) and qu (*quick*), teach these sounds by saying other words that begin with these sounds and having your students decide which key word and with which letter they begin.

- For two days each week, call out five words you want to review and lead your students to cheer for these words. Give your students plenty of practice with the illogically spelled words—*said, have, they, come,* and *what.*

- On review days, model how to write word wall words in sentences and include rhyming words they can spell based on the highlighted patterns.

- Use the final day of each week to help your students spell new words using the new words with highlighted patterns and the new beginning sounds. Use the three-column procedure described on pages 35–37. When the chart is complete, have your students write one sentence using words from the chart and word wall words.

make	will	eat
bake	hill	cheat
shake	chill	wheat
quake	kill	heat
wake		beat
rake		

Carla will beat me up the hill.

● Review the First 50 Words

When you have added the second 25 words to your wall, take a few weeks to help your students review and consolidate the word wall words and the rhyming words and teach them how to spell words with the *s* ending. Use the WORDO game to review words and teach the *s* ending. Choose 20 words and write them on index cards. Include the more difficult word wall words, rhyming words that begin with the new letters (*k, v, w, y, z, ch, sh, th, wh,* and *qu*) and some words with the *s* ending. Show your students the index cards and have them say and cheer each word. Then have them choose 9 of the 20 words to write in the squares. Remind them that to win, they must have each word spelled correctly.

said	hides	shook
have	chests	jumps
woods	children	thin

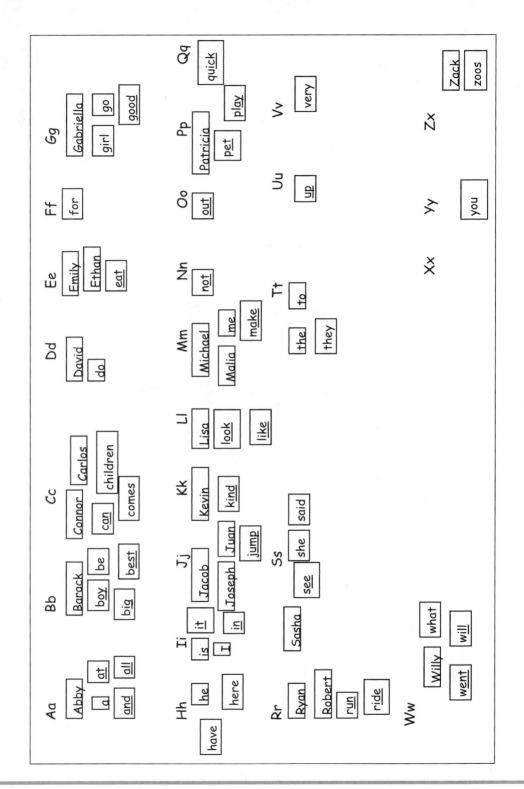

Aa Abby | a | at | and | all

Bb Barack | boy | be | big | best

Cc Connor | Carlos | can | children | comes

Dd David | do

Ee Emily | Ethan | eat

Ff for

Gg Gabriella | girl | go | good

Hh he | here | have

Ii is | it | I | in

Jj Jacob | Joseph | Juan | jump

Kk Kevin | kind

Ll Lisa | look | like

Mm Michael | Malia | me | make

Nn not

Oo out

Pp Patricia | pet | play

Qq quick

Rr Ryan | Robert | run | ride

Ss Sasha | she | see | said

Tt to | the | they

Uu up

Vv very

Xx

Yy you

Zx / Zz Zack | zoos

Ww Willy | what | went | will

Choose words from the following chart. Words followed by (*s*) can add the
s ending.

Note: New words are **bold**; rhyming patterns are highlighted.

Sets 1 and 2	b, c, d, f, g, h, j, l, m, n, p, r, s, t **k, v, w, y, z, ch, sh, th, wh, qu** **s** ending
a	
all	**ball** (s) **call** (s) **fall** (s) **hall** (s) **mall** (s) **tall** **wall** (s)
and	band (s) hand (s) land (s) sand
at	bat (s) cat (s) fat hat(s) mat (s) Nat pat (s) Pat rat (s) sat **chat** (s) **that**
be	
best	**nest** (s) **pest** (s) **rest** (s) **test** (s) **vest** (s) **west** **chest** (s) **quest** (s)
big	dig (s) fig (s) pig (s) **wig** (s)
boy (s)	joy Joy toy (s) Roy
can (s)	ban (s) dan fan (s) man Nan pan (s) ran tan **van** (s) **than**
children	
comes	
do	
eat (s)	beat (s) heat (s) meat (s) neat seat (s) **cheat** (s) **wheat**
for	
girl (s)	**whirl** (s)
go	
good	**hood** (s) **wood** (s)
have	
he	
here	
i	

in	fin (s) tin **win** (s) **chin** (s) **thin**
is	
it	**bit** (s) **fit** (s) **hit** (s) **lit** **pit** **sit** (s) **quit** (s)
jump (s)	bump (s) dump (s) hump (s) lump (s) pump (s) **thump** (s)
kind	**find** **mind** (s)
like (s)	bike (s) hike (s) mike
look (s)	book (s) cook (s) hook (s) took **shook**
make (s)	**bake** (s) **cake** (s) **fake** (s) **Jake** **lake** (s) **rake** (s) **take** (s) **wake** (s) **quake** (s) **shake** (s)
me	
not	cot (s) dot (s) got hot lot (s) pot (s) rot (s) **shot** (s)
out	**pout** (s) **shout** (s)
pet (s)	bet (s) get (s) jet (s) let net (s) set (s) **vet** **wet**
play (s)	**bay** (s) **day** (s) **Fay** **hay** **jay** **lay** **may** **pay** (s) **ray** **say** **way** (s)
quick	**Dick** **kick** (s) **lick** (s) **Mick** **Nick** **pick** (s) **Rick** **sick** **tick** (s) **thick** **chick** (s)
ride (s)	**hide** (s) **side** (s) **tide** (s) **wide**
run (s)	bun(s) fun gun (s) sun
said	
see (s)	bee (s) fee (s)
she	
the	
they	
to	
up	**cup** (s) **pup** (s)
very	
went	**bent** **dent** (s) **lent** **rent** **sent** **tent** (s) **vent** (s)

what	
will	**bill** **bill** (s) **dill** **fill** (s) **gill** (s) **hill** (s) **Jill** **kill** (s) **mill** (s) **pill** (s) **chill** (s)
you	
zoos	

You might also want to review and consolidate by using the three column chart to review new words and sounds. When the chart is complete, be sure to have everyone write one sentence using words from the chart and word wall words.

went	best	eat
sent	nest	cheat
rent	quest	wheat
vent	vest	neat
tent	west	
	chest	

I have a neat tent and the best vest in the west.

The Third 25 Words

When all your students can spell the first 50 words—and rhyming words with single consonants and digraphs—you are ready to begin adding the next 25 words:

am	are	black	bright	but	clown	crashing
did	drink	flag	friend	grow	had	her
his	price	saw	skate	sleep	smart	snap
spell	stop	swim	train			

In addition to some common words, this list contains an example for the common blends *bl, br, cl, cr, dr, fl, fr, gr, pr, sk, sl, sm, sn, sp, st, sw,* and *tr*. There are also examples for the common rhyming patterns *ack, ad, ag, ain, am, ap, art, ash, ate, aw, eep, ell, ice, id, ight, im, ink, op, ow* (grow), *own* (clown), and *ut*. The goal for this list is that your students should be able to spell all 25 words and rhyming words that begin with these blends.

If You Teach Older Children

If you teach older children, dictate the following paragraph to your students to determine which words you need on your word wall. Be sure your students are seated where they cannot see what anyone else is writing. Remember that you want to see what they can spell automatically without laboring over words, so don't tell them you are assessing their spelling needs and keep a brisk pace as you dictate.

> The *skit* is a *treat*. A **clown** and **his friend skate** to town. The **skate**s do not have *brak*es. They can not **stop** for the **train**. They hit it, **but** it is the **train** that comes **crashing** *down flat*! Wink*ing*, they *grin* at you.

Assess their spelling needs by considering the four criteria this set of words is intended to teach.

- Look at the spelling of the bold words (**clown, his, friend, skate, stop, train, but, crashing**) to determine if any of these common words are misspelled by any of your students.

- Look at the first letters in the underlined words (sk, tr, br, fl, gr) to determine if they can spell words beginning with these blends.

- Look at the italicized words (*skit, treat, brakes, down, flat, grin*) to determine if they can use common words they know to spell rhyming words that begin with blends.

- Look at *winking* and *crashing* to determine if they can spell words with the *ing* ending.

Add words needed by some of your students to the class word wall and words needed by only a few students to their personal word walls.

● Teaching These 25 Words and Patterns

The third set of words contains more high-frequency words and an example for all the common blends. The highlighted words contain a rhyming pattern your students can use to spell many other words. Another goal to accomplish while you teach this set of words is to teach your students to spell words with the *ing* ending. *Crashing* is the key word for the *ing* ending.

am	are	black	bright	but	clown	crashing
did	drink	flag	friend	grow	had	her
his	price	saw	skate	sleep	smart	snap
spell	stop	swim	train			

Use the procedures outlined for the first two sets to teach your students to spell the 25 words, the sounds for the common blends, and how to spell words that rhyme with the word wall words and begin with blends.

- Add words to the wall gradually, no more than five each week.

- On the day you add new words and the following day, lead your students to cheer three times for each new word and model the writing of each word.

- When you add the key words for the blends, teach these sounds by saying other words that begin with these sounds and having your students decide which key word they begin like and with which letters they begin.

- For two days each week, call out five words you want to review and lead your students to cheer for these words. Give your students lots of practice with the illogically spelled words *are* and *friend*.

- On review days, model how to write word wall words in sentences and include rhyming words your students can spell based on the highlighted patterns.

- Use the final day of each week to help your students spell new words using the new words with highlighted patterns and the new beginning sounds. Use the three-column procedure described in the previous section. As much as possible, choose key words with the same ending sound so that your students have to choose the word that rhymes—not just ones that end alike. Include lots of words that begin with blends in the words they decide how to spell. When each chart is complete, ask your students to write one sentence using words from the chart and word wall words.

make	black	quick
brake	track	brick
Blake	snack	stick
snake	smack	trick
	stack	click
	crack	

Blake saw a quick black snake.

not	skate	bright
plot	plate	night
slot	rate	right
spot	crate	fright
shot	state	flight

The boys and girls like to ice skate on a bright night.

all	spell	will
small	smell	grill
stall	yell	drill
mall	shell	still
	fell	spill
		skill

The small girl fell at the mall.

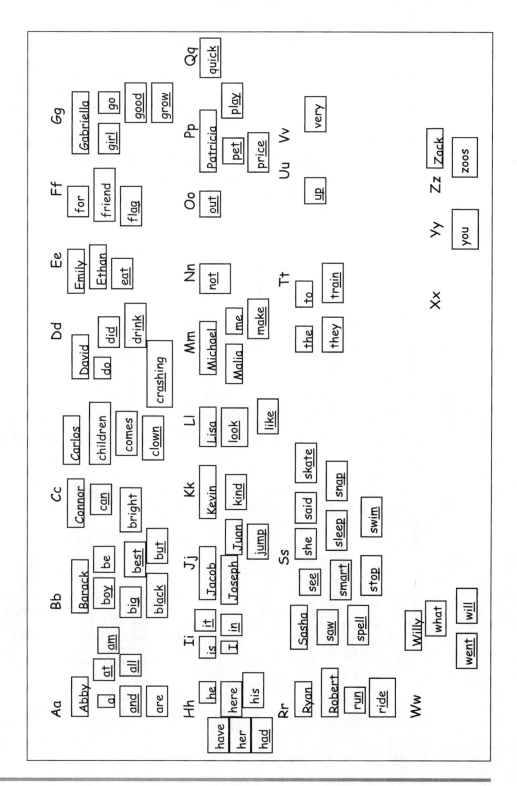

● Review the First 75 Words

When you have 75 words on your wall, take a few weeks to help your students review and consolidate the word wall words and the rhyming words and teach them how to spell words with the *ing* ending. Use the WORDO game to review words and teach the *ing* ending. Choose 20 words and write them on index cards. Include the more difficult word wall words, rhyming words that begin with blends, and some words with the *s* and *ing* endings. Show your students the index cards and have them say and cheer each word. Then have them choose 9 of the 20 words to write in the squares. Remind them that to win, they must have each word spelled correctly.

are	sleeping	drawing
brooks	thinking	crashing
cracking	flashing	friends

Choose words from the following chart. Words followed by (*ing*) can add the *ing* ending.

Note: New words are **bold**; rhyming patterns are highlighted.

Sets 1, 2, and 3	b, c, d, f, g, h, j, k, l, m, n, p, r, s, t, v, w, y, z, ch, sh, th, wh, qu **bl, br, cl, cr, dr, fl, fr, gr, pl, pr, sk, sl, sm, sn, sp, st, sw, tr** **ing** ending
a	
all	ball call (ing) fall (ing) hall mall tall wall **small stall** (ing)
am	**dam ham jam Pam ram Sam clam cram gram slam**
and	band hand land sand **brand grand stand**
are	
at	bat cat fat hat mat Nat pat Pat rat sat chat that **brat flat**
be	

best	nest (ing) pest rest test (ing) vest west chest quest
big	dig fig pig wig
black	**back Jack lack** (ing) **pack** (ing) **rack sack tack** (ing) **shack whack** (ing) **crack** (ing) **smack** (ing) **snack** (ing) **stack** (ing) **track** (ing)
boy	joy Joy Roy toy **Troy**
bright	**fight** (ing) **light** (ing) **might night right sight tight flight fright**
but	**cut gut hut nut rut shut**
can	ban Dan fan man Nan pan ran tan van than **bran clan plan Stan**
children	
clown	**down gown town brown crown drown**
comes	
crashing	**ash bash** (ing) **cash** (ing) **dash** (ing) **gash hash mash** (ing) **rash flash** (ing) **smash** (ing) **stash** (ing)
did	**bid hid kid lid rid grid skid slid**
do	
drink (ing)	**link** (ing) **pink rink sink** (ing) **wink** (ing) **think** (ing) **blink** (ing) **stink** (ing)
eat (ing)	beat (ing) heat (ing) meat neat seat cheat (ing) wheat **treat** (ing)
flag	**bag lag nag sag tag wag brag drag snag**
for	
friend	
girl	whirl (ing)
go	
good	hood wood **stood**
grow (ing)	**low mow** (ing) **row** (ing) **tow** (ing) **blow** (ing) **crow** (ing) **flow** (ing) **slow**
had	**bad dad mad pad sad Chad Brad grad**

have	
he	
her	
here	
his	
I	
in	fin tin win chin thin **grin skin spin**
is	
it	bit fit hit kit lit pit sit quit **grit skit slit spit**
jump (ing)	bump (ing) dump (ing) hump lump pump (ing) thump(ing) **clump grump plump slump stump**
kind	find (ing) mind (ing) **blind grind** (ing)
like	bike hike Mike **spike**
look (ing)	book cook (ing) hook took shook **brook Brook crook**
make	bake cake fake Jake lake rake take wake quake shake **Blake brake snake**
me	
not	cot dot got hot lot pot rot shot **plot slot spot**
out	pout (ing) shout (ing) **snout spout** (ing) **trout**
pet	bet get jet let net set vet wet
play (ing)	bay day Fay hay Jay lay (ing) may May pay (ing) Ray say (ing) way **clay gray pray** (ing) **stay** (ing)
price	**ice dice lice mice nice rice slice spice**
quick	Dick kick (ing) lick (ing) Mick Nick pick (ing) Rick sick tick (ing) thick chick **brick click** (ing) **stick** (ing) **trick** (ing)
ride	hide side tide wide **bride pride slide**
run	bun fun gun sun **spun**
said	
saw	**jaw law paw raw thaw claw draw** (ing) **slaw**
see (ing)	bee fee **flee** (ing) **free** (ing) **tree**

she	
skate	**date gate hate Kate late mate Nate rate crate plate state**
sleep (ing)	**beep** (ing) **deep jeep keep** (ing) **peep** (ing) **weep** (ing) **sheep creep** (ing) **steep**
smart	**art Bart cart dart** (ing) **mart part chart start** (ing)
snap	**cap gap lap map nap rap sap tap clap flap trap zap**
spell (ing)	**bell fell Nell tell** (ing) **well yell** (ing) **shell** (ing) **smell** (ing)
stop	**cop hop mop pop top shop chop drop flop plop prop**
swim	**dim him Jim Kim rim Tim brim slim skim trim**
the	
they	
to	
train	**main pain rain** (ing) **chain brain drain** (ing) **grain plain stain**
up	cup pup
very	
went	bent dent lent rent (ing) sent tent vent **Brent Trent**
what	
will (ing)	Bill bill (ing) dill fill (ing) gill hill Jill kill (ing) mill pill Will chill **drill** (ing) **grill** (ing) **skill spill** (ing) **still**
you	
zoos	

You're the Expert!

I may be the expert on spelling but you are the expert on your students! When deciding which words to include in all the lists, I tried to include only words that most young children would have in their listening vocabularies and that you could help them connect meaning for by putting the word in a sentence. I also used this criterion to decide which words could add the *s, ing,* and *ed* ending. I included the word *willing* because I thought most children would understand the word in a sentence such as, "Kevin was willing to share his toys with his cousin." I did not include other words such as *chilling* or *booking* because I couldn't think of a sentence that would clue young children to their meaning. I also decided to leave the teaching of spelling changes until the second 100 words and thus did not include any words that required a spelling change when adding the *ing* and *ed* ending. But, remember, you are the expert on your kids. Omit from all my lists words to which your students cannot connect meanings and add any you think they might know. Look at the lists throughout the chapter as starting points for customizing your own list of words. If you think your students are ready to master spelling changes as they learn *ing* and *ed* endings, you can find lots of words in the lists to teach this complex concept.

100 Magic Words

When all your students can spell the key words in the first three sets and are making progress toward spelling rhyming words with consonants, digraphs, and blends, you are ready to begin working toward 100 words by gradually adding these words:

coat	each	flew	from	has	how	if
little	made	my	of	old	on	so
some	talk	there	thing	this	wanted	was
we	when	with	your			

This list contains many words that are not spelled logically, including *from, of, some, there, want, was,* and *your*. There are also examples for the common rhyming patterns *ade, alk, each, en, ew, ing, oat, old, ow* (how), and *y* (my). The goal for this list is that your students should be able to spell all 25 words and rhyming words that begin with consonants, digraphs, and blends. If you teach first grade, this set is the final set of words. First-graders who end the year able to spell all 100 words and some words that rhyme with these words are well on their way to becoming excellent spellers. You will see their excellence reflected in the eagerness and fluency they demonstrate in their writing.

If You Teach Older Children

If you teach older children, dictate the following paragraph to your students to determine which words your students need to spell. Be sure your students are seated where they cannot see what anyone else is writing. Remember that you want to see what they can spell automatically without laboring over words, so don't tell them you are assessing their spelling and keep a brisk pace as you dictate.

> The *sky* look<u>ed</u> like *chalk*. The *crew* did not see the *beach*. **When** the *cold blew* in, they **wanted** to *reach* land, but did not see **how** to get **there**. *Then* **some of** the **old** *men* saw a **little** *dry* sand and jump<u>ed</u> **from** the *boat* to *wade* in. The rest **made** it **when** they *float*<u>ed</u> in **with** the tide.

Assess their spelling needs by considering the three criteria this set of words is intended to teach.

- Look at the spelling of the bold words (**when, wanted, how, there, some, of, old, little, from, made, when, with**) to determine if any of these common words are misspelled by any of your students.

- Look at the italicized words (*sky, chalk, crew. beach, cold, blew, reach, then, men, dry, boat, wade, float*) to determine if they can use common words they know to spell rhyming words.

- Look at *looked, jumped,* and *floated* to determine if they can spell words with the *ed* ending.

Add words needed by some students to your class word wall and words needed by only a few students to their personal word walls.

● Teaching These 25 Words and Patterns

This set of words contains more high-frequency words and words that contain a rhyming pattern your students can use to spell many other words. Another goal to accomplish while you teach this set of words is to teach your students to spell words with the *ed* ending. *Wanted* is the key word for the *ed* ending.

coat	each	flew	from	has	how	if
little	made	my	of	old	on	so
some	talk	there	thing	this	wanted	was
we	when	with	your			

Use the procedures outlined for the first three sets to teach your students to spell these 25 words, and how to spell words that rhyme with the word wall words.

- Add words to the wall gradually, no more than five each week.
- On the day you add new words and the following day, lead your students to cheer three times for each new word and model the writing of each word.
- For two days each week, call out five words you want to review and lead your students to cheer for these words. Give your students plenty of practice with the illogically spelled words—*from, of, some, there, want, was, where,* and *your.*
- On review days, model how to write word wall words in sentences and include rhyming words they can spell based on the highlighted patterns.
- Use the final day of each week to help your students spell new words using the new words with highlighted patterns and the new beginning sounds. Use the three-column procedure described in the previous section. As much as possible, choose key words with the same ending sound so that your students have to choose the word that rhymes—not just ones that end alike. Include lots of words that begin with digraphs and blends in the words they decide how to spell. When each chart is complete, have your students write one sentence using words from the chart and word wall words.

made	ride	did
blade	bride	slid
shade	pride	skid
grade	slide	grid
trade		hid
Jade		

Jade slid down the slide and then hid from her friends.

flew	how	saw
drew	now	draw
chew	plow	slaw
new	chow	claw
grew		thaw
stew		

Do you like to eat stew and slaw?

my	play	boy
try	gray	toy
fry	clay	joy
fly	stay	Troy
dry	tray	
sky		

Troy has a new toy that can fly in the sky.

When you have all 100 words on your wall, take a few weeks to help your students review and consolidate the word wall words and the rhyming words and teach them how to spell words with the *ed* ending. Use the WORDO game to review words and teach the *ed* ending. Choose 20 words and write them on index cards. Include the more difficult word wall words, rhyming words, and some words with the *s, ing,* and *ed* endings. Show your students the index cards and have them say and cheer each word. Then have them choose 9 of the 20 words to write in the squares. Remind them that to win, they must have each word spelled correctly.

there	wanted	throat
walked	from	chewed
chewing	coats	friends

Choose words from the following chart. Words followed by (*ed*) can add the *ed* ending.

Note: New words are **bold**; rhyming patterns are highlighted.

Sets 1, 2, 3, and 4	b, c, d, f, g, h, j, k, l, m, n, p, r, s, t, v, w, y, z, ch, sh, th, wh, qu bl, br, cl, cr, dr, fl, fr, gr, pl, pr, sk, sl, sm, sn, sp, st, sw, tr **ed** ending
a	
all	ball call (ed) fall hall mall tall wall small stall (ed)
am	Dam ham jam Pam ram Sam clam cram gram slam
and	band hand (ed) land (ed) sand brand grand stand
are	
at	bat cat fat hat mat Nat pat Pat rat sat chat that brat flat
be	
best	nest (ed) pest test (ed) vest west chest quest
big	dig fig pig rig wig
black	back Jack lack (ed) pack (ed) rack sack tack (ed) shack whack(ed) crack (ed) smack (ed) snack stack (ed) track (ed)
boy	joy Joy Roy toy Troy
bright	fight light (ed) might night right sight tight fright
but	cut gut hut nut rut shut
can	ban Dan fan man Nan pan ran tan van than bran clan plan Stan
children	
clown	down gown town brown crown drown
comes	
coat	**boat float** (ed) **goat throat**
crashing	ash bash cash (ed) dash (ed) gash hash mash (ed) rash flash (ed) smash (ed) stash (ed)
did	bid hid kid lid rid grid skid slid

do	
drink	link (ed) pink rink sink wink (ed) think blink (ed) stink
each	**beach peach reach** (ed) **teach**
eat	beat heat (ed) meat neat seat cheat (ed) wheat
flag	bag lag nag sag tag wag brag drag snag
flew	**few new chew** (ed) **blew crew drew grew stew**
for	
friend	
from	
girl	whirl (ed)
go	
good	hood wood stood
grow	low mow (ed) row (ed) tow (ed) blow crow flow (ed) slow
had	bad dad mad pad sad Chad Brad grad
has	
have	
he	
her	
here	
his	
how	**bow** (ed) **cow now wow chow plow** (ed)
I	
if	
in	fin pin tin win chin thin grin skin spin
is	
it	bit fit hit kit lit pit sit quit grit skit slit spit
jump (ed)	bump (ed) dump (ed) hump lump pump (ed) thump (ed) clump grump plump slump stump

kind	find mind (ed) blind grind
like	bike hike Mike spike
little	
look (ed)	book cook (ed) hook (ed) took shook brook Brook crook
made	**fade Jade wade shade blade grade trade**
make	bake cake fake Jake lake rake take wake quake shake Blake brake snake
me	
my	**by shy why cry dry fry fly pry sky sly spy try**
not	cot dot got hot lot pot rot shot plot slot spot trot
of	
old	**bold cold fold** (ed) **gold hold sold told**
on	
out	pout (ed) shout (ed) snout spout trout
pet	bet get jet let net set vet wet
play (ed)	bay day Fay hay Jay lay may May pay (ed) Ray say way clay gray pray (ed) stay (ed)
price	ice dice lice mice nice rice slice spice
quick	Dick kick (ed) lick (ed) Mick Nick pick (ed) Rick sick tick (ed) thick chick brick click (ed) stick trick (ed)
ride	hide side tide wide bride pride slide
run	bun fun gun sun spun
said	
saw	jaw law paw raw thaw (ed) claw (ed) draw slaw
see	bee fee flee free glee tree
she	
skate	date gate hate Kate late mate Nate rate crate plate state
sleep	beep (ed) deep jeep keep peep weep sheep creep steep
smart	art Bart cart dart (ed) mart part chart start (ed)

sn**ap**	cap gap lap map nap rap sap tap clap flap trap zap
so	
some	
sp**ell** (ed)	bell fell Nell tell well yell (ed) shell smell (ed)
st**op**	cop hop mop pop top shop chop drop flop plop prop
sw**im**	dim him Jim Kim rim Tim brim skim slim trim
talk (ed)	**walk** (ed) **chalk** **stalk**
the	
there	
they	
thing	**ding king ring sing wing bring fling sling sting swing**
this	
to	
tr**ain**	main pain rain (ed) chain brain drain (ed) grain plain stain (ed)
up	cup pup
very	
wanted	
was	
we	
w**ent**	bent dent (ed) lent rent (ed) sent tent vent Brent Trent
what	
when	**Ben den hen Jen Ken men pen ten then**
wi**ll**	Bill bill dill fill (ed) gill hill Jill kill (ed) mill pill Will chill drill (ed) grill (ed) skill spill (ed) still
with	
you	
your	
zoos	

Review, Consolidate, Celebrate!

If your students can spell the 100 words on your wall and words with the same rhyming pattern, they should now be able to spell over 600 words. If they can add *s, ed,* and *ing* to some of these 600 words, their spelling vocabulary should be almost 1,000 words! In addition, they should be able to spell the names of their classmates and be automatic at capitalizing the first letter of people's names. Take as much time as you can in the final weeks of school to review the words, help them consolidate their spelling strategies, and celebrate their spelling prowess!

● WORDO

If your students have enjoyed playing WORDO throughout the year, you can now graduate them to the "big" version of WORDO. Make WORDO sheets with 25 squares. If you like, put WORDO in the center square.

		WORDO		

Choose 30 to 40 words and write them on index cards. Include word wall words, your children's names, words that rhyme with word wall words and words, with the *s, ed,* and *ing* endings. Show the children your 30 to 40 words and have them do a quick cheer for each word. Then, give them time to choose and write words on their WORDO sheet to fill up all the spaces. Remind them that they should write each word very carefully because to win, they must have words covered that were called and each word must be spelled correctly—including beginning with a capital letter if it is someone's name. Shuffle your index cards and call out words. When someone wins, check his or her sheet. If the child has the correct words covered and all are spelled correctly, have everyone clear their cards and play another round or two. The next time you play, choose a different 30 to 40 words so that you provide review with all the word wall words and patterns.

● Be a Mind Reader

Be a Mind Reader is another game you can use to review word wall words. In this game, you think of a word on the wall and then give five clues to that word. Choose a word and write it on a scrap of paper but do not let the students see what word you have written. Tell each student to number a piece of paper from 1 to 5. Explain that you are going to see who can read your mind and figure out which of the words on the wall you are thinking of and have written on your paper. Tell them you will give them five clues. By the fifth clue, everyone should guess your word, but if they read your mind they might get it before the fifth clue. Since you now have 100 words on your wall and your students' names, give a first clue which limits the words to 6 or 7 alphabet letters. Tell your students to write next to number 1 the word they think it might be. Each succeeding clue should narrow down what it can be until by clue 5 there is only one possible word. As you give clues, students write the word they believe it is next to each number. If succeeding clues confirm the word a student has written next to one number, the student writes that word again by the next number. If succeeding clues eliminate the word, students choose a new word that fits all the clues.

After clue 5, show students the word you wrote on your scrap paper and say, "I know you all have the word next to number 5 but who has it next to number 4? 3? 2? 1?" All students who guessed the word on line 1 are the winners. If no one guessed it on line 1, the winners are everyone who guessed it on line 2. In the unlikely event that no one guessed it on line 1 or 2, the winners are everyone who guessed it on line 3. Once you have your winners, check their papers to make sure the word is spelled correctly every time. If someone has not spelled the word correctly, he or she does not win! Here are some examples to get you started.

1. It's a word wall word that starts with *a, b, c, d, e,* or *f.*
2. It has 5 letters.
3. It does not have a *b.*
4. It begins with *c.*
5. This is someone you would see at the circus.

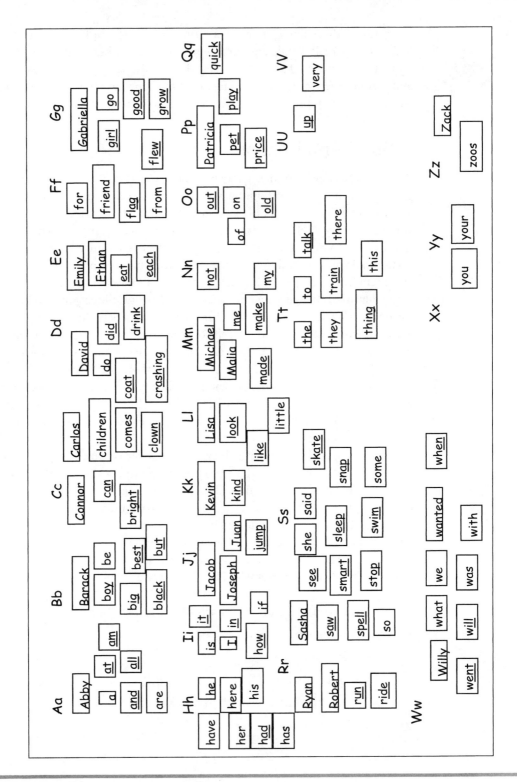

1. It's a word wall word that starts with *u, v, w, x, y,* or *z.*
2. It has 4 letters.
3. It begins with *w.*
4. It ends with *t.*
5. You use this word to ask a question.

1. It's a word wall word that starts with *g, h, i, j, k,* or *l.*
2. It is the name of someone in this class.
3. It begins with *J.*
4. It has more than 4 letters.
5. This name ends with a *b.*

1. It's a word wall word that starts with *p, q, r, s,* or *t.*
2. It has 5 letters.
3. It begins with *s.*
4. It is something you can do.
5. You can do this on the sidewalk, on ice, or at the skating rink.

● Ruler Tap

Ruler Tap is a simple activity but children love it and it does help them review the words. Begin the game by saying a word wall word and tapping the ruler for several of the letters (without saying them). When you stop tapping, call on a student to finish spelling the word out loud. If that student correctly finishes spelling the word, give the ruler to that student and let him or her say a word and tap some of the letters. That student calls on another student and if that student correctly finishes spelling the word, he or she gets the ruler and the game continues!

Chapter 4

More Common Patterns and Words Including Common Contractions and Homophones

This chapter contains lists, diagnostic paragraphs, and activities for teaching the second 100 most important words all elementary students need to be able to spell. Like the first 100 words, these words are divided into four sets of 25 each. If you teach second or third grade, these 100 words are probably the ones most appropriate for your grade. Regardless of what grade level you teach, the activities in this chapter assume that your students have mastered the 100 words from the previous chapter and can use beginning letter sounds and rhyming patterns to spell hundreds of other words. Here are the first 100 words with spelling patterns highlighted. If your students cannot spell these words and words with the same rhyming patterns, cycle back through Chapter 3.

The First 100 Words				
a	all	am	and	are
at	be	best	big	black
boy	bright	but	can	children
clown	coat	comes	crashing	did
do	drink	each	eat	flag
flew	for	friend	from	girl
go	good	grow	had	has
have	he	her	here	his
how	I	if	in	is
it	jump	kind	like	little
look	made	make	me	my
not	of	old	on	out
pet	play	price	quick	ride
run	said	saw	see	she
skate	sleep	smart	snap	so
some	spell	stop	swim	talk
the	there	they	thing	this
to	train	up	very	wanted
was	we	went	what	when
will	with	you	your	zoos

Regardless of grade level, begin your word wall with the names of your students. Having their names there will help your students view the word wall positively and allows you to review the important spelling skill of capitalizing the first letter of names of people. After you have the names there and the cheering/ writing procedures established, you can gradually add other words. The 100 words in this chapter are divided into four sets of 25 each. Each set contains some common, illogically spelled, high-frequency words (*because, great, always*) and some key words for rhyming patterns (*spoke, street, weekend*). Your students will also learn to spell common contractions (*can't, I'm, what's*), homophones (*to, two, too; no, know*) and compound words (*homework, birthday*). This set of words also includes words that will teach them the spelling changes required when *s, ed,* and *ing* are added to some words (*swimming; families, tried*). Capitalization skills are extended beyond people's names to include place names and holidays.

The Second 100 Words				
about	after	again	almost	also
always	animal	aren't	around	because
bedroom	before	birthday	brother	build
busy	campfire	can't	catches	city
could	cousin	does	don't	*families*
family	favorite	*flies*	football	funny
getting	*glasses*	*goes*	great	holiday
homework	hundred	I'll	I'm	into
it's	know	laugh	many	**Monday**
myself	no	off	once	outside
over	people	place	pretty	really
right	**Saturday**	school	shouldn't	sister
skateboard	spoke	sport	stopped	street
summer	surprise	*swimming*	teacher	thank
Thanksgiving	their	there	they're	to
tomorrow	too	*tried*	two	under
until	*used*	wasn't	we're	wear

weekend	were	what's	where	who
why	winter	*wishes*	without	write
writing	**teacher name**	**school name**	**street name**	**city/town name**

If you teach older students, paragraphs are included that you can dictate to your students to determine which words you need to add to the wall. It is very important to use the paragraph dictation rather than a traditional spelling test to make this determination. Remember from Chapter 1 that our brains can do many automatic things and only one non-automatic thing at a time. If you simply dictate the words in spelling test form, many students will spell words correctly that they will then spell incorrectly when they are writing. You want your students to become so automatic at spelling words that they spell them correctly when they are writing and their conscious attention is allocated where it should be—that is, communicating their ideas with vivid, specific words.

The First 25 Words

The first set of 25 words includes some words with rhyming patterns that help students spell other words, some common words many second- and third-graders misspell, and examples for the spelling change of doubling consonants.

about	after	again	around	because	before	could
does	funny	laugh	many	off	over	pretty
spoke	sport	thank	under	until	were	who
why	getting	stopped	swimming			

Do Your Older Students Need Any of These Words?

If you teach older children, you need to decide which, if any, of these words to include. To determine if your students need any of these key words, dictate the following paragraph to them and have them write it without any help from you.

The **pretty** *spotted* cat *plopped* on the mat. **After** Chad *petted* her, she *napped* **until** he was *shutting* the gate. **Because** it *slammed*, she went *running* **off again**.

(continued)

Before dictating the paragraph to your students, be sure they are seated where they can't see each other's papers. Tell them you want to see what writing skills they need to work on and they should just do the best they can. Do not tell them you are assessing their spelling. If they ask you how to spell a word, simply tell them to "do the best you can." Keep a reasonable pace in your dictation—giving them enough time to get the words down but not enough to labor over the spelling of each word. Remember, you are trying to get a snapshot of their spelling proficiency while writing so that you can determine which words need to be a part of your word wall and spelling instruction.

- Look at the spelling of the bold words (**pretty, after, until, because, off, again**) to determine if any of these common words are misspelled by any of your students. The bold words are often misspelled by older children.
- Look at the underlined words (plo<u>pp</u>ed, shu<u>tt</u>ing, petted, na<u>pp</u>ed, shu<u>tt</u>ing, sla<u>mm</u>ed, ru<u>nn</u>ing) to determine if they know that you double the consonant if a word ends in a single consonant and you are adding the *ing* or *ed* ending.

If you determine that some of your students need any of these words, add these words to your wall—adding no more than five words each week and doing the activities described in this chapter to teach the words, doubling rule, and rhyming patterns. When you have added the words you determined you need and provided lots of practice with those words, dictate the paragraph to them again. If only a few of your students need some of the words, create a personal word wall for those students and add a few words each week to their personal word wall. Be sure they have their file folder word wall out while writing and hold them accountable in their writing for words on the class word wall and their personal word walls.

● Teaching the Words, Doubling Rule, and Rhyming Patterns

Add these words gradually to your wall—no more than five each week. You can choose the order, but it is probably best to add the words that are key words for the doubling principle in the same week.

about	after	again	around	because	before	could
does	funny	laugh	many	off	pretty	spoke
sport	thank	over	under	until	were	who
why	getting	stopped	swimming			

On the day you add words, have your students use these words in oral sentences to make sure they can associate meaning with the words. Get your students out of their seats and lead them to cheer for the five words—three times each word. Have them say the word they are cheering at the beginning and end.

"after a-f-t-e-r; a-f-t-e-r; a-f-t-e-r; after"

"before b-e-f-o-r-e; b-e-f-o-r-e; b-e-f-o-r-e; before"

"laugh l-a-u-g-h; l-a-u-g-h; l-a-u-g-h; laugh"

"off o-f-f; o-f-f; o-f-f; off"

"were w-e-r-e; w-e-r-e; w-e-r-e; were"

Next, have them write the words as you model correct letter formation.

after

before

laugh

off

were

For the next several days, continue to lead your students to cheer for and write these words. When they have written the words in a list for two or three days, dictate a few sentences for them to write and model how to use these words in sentences. Use the five new words, words they should know from the first 100 words, and names of your students. Include some of the new words with *ed, s,* and *ing* endings (without spelling changes).

Demonte and Jacob were playing ball.

Jacob hit the ball and Demonte ran after it.

Paula laughed when the clown fell off the bike.

Carlos got here before Drew.

When all your students can spell these five words quickly and automatically, add five more words. Say some sentences using the new words to make sure your students have these in their oral vocabulary. Lead your students to cheer the new words—three times each:

"under u-n-d-e-r; u-n-d-e-r; u-n-d-e-r; under"

"over o-v-e-r; o-v-e-r; o-v-e-r; over"

"swimming s-w-i-m-m-i-n-g; s-w-i-m-m-i-n-g; s-w-i-m-m-i-n-g; swimming"

"getting g-e-t-t-i-n-g; g-e-t-t-i-n-g; g-e-t-t-i-n-g; getting"

"stopped s-t-o-p-p-e-d; s-t-o-p-p-e-d; s-t-o-p-p-e-d; stopped"

Model how to write the new words and have the students write them.

under

over

swimming

getting

stopped

Focus on these five new words for two or three days. Then spend two or three days reviewing the old words. Each day lead your students to cheer for five words but include some old words and some new words. Dictate a few sentences for your students to write that include word wall words, words and rhyming words from the first 100 words, and the names of your students.

Pablo stopped to pick up his friend, Jack.

Do you go swimming at the beach?

Matthew might be getting a new pet.

Continue to add five words each week following these procedures for each group of words.

- Use new words in sentences to make sure your students have the words in their oral vocabulary.
- For two days, focus only on the new words by leading your students to cheer for and write the new words.
- For three days, choose five words to cheer, including some old words and some new words.
- Model sentences for your students to write that include new and old words.

● Review the First 25 Words

When you have all 25 words on your wall, take a few weeks to consolidate your word wall words and sounds by letting your students play a few rounds of WORDO. Make copies of a sheet with 9 squares. Have your children choose 9 of the 25 words and write them—one to a square. Meanwhile, make yourself a deck of calling cards by writing the 25 words on index cards—one to a card. When your students have their WORDO sheets ready, shuffle your cards and call out words until someone has covered all the words on his or her card. The first person to

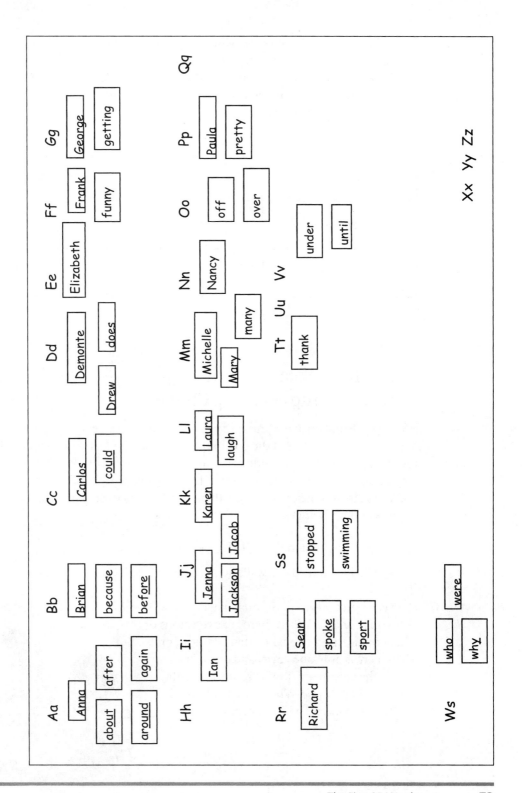

Aa
ab<u>out</u>
a<u>round</u>
<u>Anna</u>
after
again

Bb
Brian
because
be<u>fore</u>

Cc
Carlos
c<u>ould</u>

Dd
Demonte
<u>Drew</u>
<u>does</u>

Ee
Elizabeth

Ff
Frank
funny

Gg
George
getting

Hh
Ii
Ian

Jj
<u>Jenna</u>
Jackson Jacob

Kk
Karen

Ll
<u>Laura</u>
laugh

Mm
Michelle
<u>Mary</u>
many

Nn
Nancy

Oo
off
over

Pp
Paula
pretty

Qq

Rr
Richard
Sean
spoke
sport

Ss
stopped
swimming

Tt Uu Vv
thank
under
until

Ws
who
wh<u>y</u>
<u>were</u>

Xx Yy Zz

cover the card completely is the winner and should shout, "WORDO." Check to see that all the words the winner covered were called and they are all spelled correctly. If you have time, have the students clear their cards and play another round. Using Cheerios or some other nutritious cereal to cover the words makes for quick clean-up and a nutritious snack!

getting	over	laugh
spoke	pretty	many
stopped	could	until

● Teaching Your Students the Doubling Spelling Change

When your students have learned to spell *swimming, getting,* and *stopped,* help them to notice that the letters at the end of the words *swim, get,* and *stop* are doubled when the endings *ed* and *ing* are added. Tell them that we only double the letter when one vowel is followed by one consonant. If there are two vowels or two consonants, we don't double the consonant. Show them some words with endings that don't require spelling changes.

looked	cooking	landed	testing	crashed	smashing	started
spelling	talked	walking	ringing	spilled	grilling	

Help your students to notice that in all these words, there are either two vowels or two consonants. When there are two vowels or two consonants, don't double the consonant when adding *ed* or *ing.* But when there is only one vowel and one consonant, double the consonant. (Some teachers call this the *1 plus 1 plus 1 rule.* When we have 1 vowel and 1 consonant, we add 1 consonant.)

Give your students practice doubling the consonant, when appropriate, by having them write these 10 words on a piece of paper. Write these same words on your board or chart.

bump

walk

shop

want

trim

beep

call

trap

bat

flip

Ask your students to add *ing* or *ed* to these words to spell the following words. Before they add the ending, ask them if the word they are adding to has just one consonant and one vowel or has two consonants or vowels. Write the word on your board or chart after they write it and have them check their spelling.

bumped

walking

shopping

wanted

trimmed

beeped

calling

trapped

batted

flipping

Use the WORDO game to provide more practice with this tricky spelling principle. Write 24 words on index cards. Have your students help you decide whether or not to double the consonant and have them choose squares on their WORDO sheet to write the words in. Shuffle the cards and call out the words. To win, students need to have a column, row, or diagonal covered and, of course, have to have all words correctly spelled. (Choose words from the examples listed earlier and the words next to *swimming, getting,* and *stopped* in the Set 1 chart.)

looked	slammed	smashing	talked	setting
trotting	cooking	petted	crammed	spilled
zapped	betting	WORDO	landed	napping
grilling	hopping	clapped	crashed	testing
chopping	dropped	snapped	quitting	dimmed

● Teaching Your Students to Spell Rhyming Words

When your students can spell these 25 words, help them extend their spelling skills to spelling words that rhyme with word wall words. This chart lists the rhyming words your students should be able to spell.

Note: New words are **bold**; rhyming patterns are highlighted.

Set 1	Words they should be able to spell
about	pout scout shout snout spout sprout trout **blackout cookout dropout handout tryout**
after	
again	
around	**bound found ground hound mound pound round sound background aground**
because	

before	bore chore core more score shore store tore wore ashore ignore restore outscore
could	would . should
does	
funny	bunny sunny
laugh	
many	
off	
over	
pretty	
spoke	broke choke Coke joke poke smoke stroke woke awoke heatstroke sunstroke
sport	fort port short sort report deport import
thank	bank blank crank drank Frank plank prank rank sank spank tank yank outrank
under	
until	
were	
who	
why	by shy why cry dry fry fly pry sky sly spy try standby rely deny
getting	batted batting chatted chatting patted patting betted betting petted petting setting hitting quitting spitting trotted trotting cutting shutting
swimming	crammed cramming rammed ramming slammed slamming dimmed dimming trimmed trimming
stopped	napped napping clapped clapping rapped, rapping, snapped snapping slapped slapping zapped zapping chipped chipping dipped dipping flipped flipping nipped ripped sipped sipping shipped shipping tipped tripped chopped chopping dropped dropping flopped flopping hopped hopping plopped plopping popped popping shopped shopping stopping topped topping

To teach your students to use the words they know to figure out how to spell other words, you can use the following lesson format. Give the children a sheet of paper that looks like this. Create the same sheet for you to write on using your board or chart paper.

Choose three words from this list and from the first 100 words that have similar rhyming patterns. Demonstrate for them how to underline or highlight the rhyming pattern in each word.

spoke	thank	drink

Say some words that rhyme with *spoke, thank,* and *drink* and use each word in a sentence.

"stroke   The man suffered a stroke and was rushed to the hospital."

"blink   Try not to blink when I take the photo."

Next, have your students pronounce each word and tell you which word it rhymes with, then write it in the appropriate column. After they write each word, ask them to underline or highlight the rhyming pattern and notice that they are the same. Include several words in which they can already spell the first syllable, and the last syllable rhymes with one of the three words. When the chart is finished, have them notice that the three words they know helped them spell 12 more words—including some longer words!

spoke	thank	drink
joke	blank	blink
broke	prank	stink
awoke	Frank	shrink
stroke		rethink
sunstroke		

To make sure they understand that you want them to use these rhyming spelling patterns when they are writing, model how to write a sentence that uses a few of the rhyming words and some word wall words. Have your students write a sentence using at least two of the rhyming words.

Frank likes to tell jokes and play pranks.

Spelling Skills Help Only if the Students Use Them When They Write!

The only reason your children need to learn how to spell words is to enable them to write fluently and well. If they learn to spell words during your spelling practice but do not spell them correctly when writing, your spelling practice is wasted. Provide weekly practice spelling the word wall words as they write a few sentences. When they are writing throughout the day, remind them to use the word wall and hold them accountable for spelling word wall words correctly in everything they write.

Do similar lessons with all the new rhyming patterns.

around	could	old
ground	would	sold
round	should	gold
found		scold
hound		fold
mound		told

Jennifer found an old hound dog.

before	sport	smart
shore	short	part
chore	fort	dart
store	port	Bart
restore	report	start

Bart starts his chores after school.

You can also use the WORDO game to help students practice rhyming words. Write 24 words that rhyme with word wall words on index cards and have the students choose where to write them on the WORDO sheet. Shuffle and call the words. Be sure the words are spelled correctly when someone wins WORDO.

bunny	would	cookout	background	ignore
should	short	standby	spy	spank
sound	score	WORDO	smoke	fort
ground	sprout	dropout	scout	crank
outrank	yank	deny	blank	rely

The Second 25 Words

When all your students can spell the first 25 word wall words and most of your children can spell rhyming words and use the doubling rule correctly, you are ready to begin working with the second set. The second set of 25 words contains 12 common words that many students have difficulty spelling:

brother	sister	people	cousin	family	animal
favorite	hundred	place	great	build	busy

Three key words are included to teach the spelling change that when a word ends in *y*, you change the *y* to *i* and then add *es* or *ed*.

families   flies   tried

To teach your students to capitalize the names of specific people, places and holidays, include the specific key words as well as the general words:

teacher	your name
city	the name of your city or town
street	the name of the street or road your school is on
school	the name of your school
holiday	Thanksgiving

The key words in this list will also allow you to teach four new rhyming patterns: *ace* (place); *ool* (school); *ed* (hundred); and *eet* (street).

If You Teach Older Children

If you teach older children, you need to decide which, if any, of these words to include. Many second-graders and older children misspell the common illogical words such as *cousin, favorite,* and *people.* Other children do not use the *y* to *i* spelling change nor do they capitalize specific nouns. Dictate the following paragraph and have students write it.

My **family** rents on *Ash* **Street** next to *King* **School** in *Lake* **City**. Like many **people** and **famil**<u>ies</u>, they keep **busy**. My **brother** <u>fries</u> clams. My **sister** <u>dries</u> figs. My **cousin** <u>tried</u> to **build** beach huts, but now he <u>flies</u> jets.

Seat your students so that they cannot see what anyone else is writing. Tell them that you want to assess their writing and they should do the best they can. Keep a reasonable pace that does not allow them to labor over the spelling of words. Assess their spelling needs by considering the three criteria this set of words is intended to teach.

- Look at the spelling of the bold words (**cousin, street, school, city, people, busy, brother, sister, cousin, build**) to determine if your students know how to spell these illogically spelled common words.

- Look at the underlined words (famil<u>ies</u>, fr<u>ies</u>, dr<u>ies</u>, tr<u>ied</u>, fl<u>ies</u>) to determine if they know the *y* to *i* spelling change.

- Look at the italicized words (*Ash, Street, King, School, Lake, City*) to determine if they spell specific words with capital letters.

If you determine that some of your students need any of these words, add whichever words they need—adding no more than five words each week. When you have added the words you determined they need and provided lots of practice with those words, dictate the paragraph to them again. If only a few of your students need any of these words, add those words to their personal word walls.

● Teaching the Words, y to i Rule, and Capitalizing Specific Names

Add these words gradually to your wall—no more than five each week. You may choose the order, but it is probably best to add the words that are key words for the *y* to *i* change in the same week. You may want to spread out the key words for the capitalizing of specific names across the weeks but be sure to include the parallel examples (holiday, Thanksgiving; school, school name, etc.) in the same week.

animal	brother	build	busy	cousin	city		families
family	favorite	flies	great	holiday	hundred		people
place	school	sister	street	teacher	Thanksgiving		tried

specific teacher name, school name, street name, and city (town) name

On the day you add words, tell your students to use these words in oral sentences to make sure they can associate meaning with the words. Get your students out of their seats and lead them to cheer for the five words—three times each word. Have them say the word they are cheering at the beginning and end.

"favorite f-a-v-o-r-i-t-e; f-a-v-o-r-i-t-e; f-a-v-o-r-i-t-e; favorite"

"people p-e-o-p-l-e; p-e-o-p-l-e; p-e-o-p-l-e; people"

"animal a-n-i-m-a-l; a-n-i-m-a-l; a-n-i-m-a-l; animal"

"holiday h-o-l-i-d-a-y; h-o-l-i-d-a-y; h-o-l-i-d-a-y; holiday"

"Thanksgiving capital T-h-a-n-k-s-g-i-v-i-n-g; capital T-h-a-n-k-s-g-i-v-i-n-g; capital T-h-a-n-k-s-g-i-v-i-n-g; Thanksgiving"

Next, have them write the words as you model correct letter formation.

animal

people

favorite

holiday

Thanksgiving

Focus on these five new words for two days. Each day, ask the children to explain why *Thanksgiving* begins with a capital letter but holiday does not. They should be able to explain that Thanksgiving is a specific holiday. Ask them to name some other specific holidays they would begin with a capital letter (Christmas, Halloween, and others). Then spend three days reviewing the old words. Each day lead your students to cheer for five words but include some of the old words and some new words. Dictate a few sentences for your students to write that include word wall words, key words, and rhyming words from the first 100 words, and students' names.

What is your favorite holiday?

Thanksgiving is my favorite holiday.

Do you have a favorite animal?

Jon likes big animals but Paulo likes little animals.

When all your students can spell the first five words quickly and automatically, add five more words. Say some sentences using the new words to make sure your students have these words in their oral vocabulary. Lead your students to cheer the new words—three times each:

"families f-a-m-i-l-i-e-s; f-a-m-i-l-i-e-s; f-a-m-i-l-i-e-s; families"

"flies f-l-i-e-s; f-l-i-e-s; f-l-i-e-s; flies"

"tried t-r-i-e-d; t-r-i-e-d; t-r-i-e-d; tried"

"school s-c-h-o-o-l; s-c-h-o-o-l; s-c-h-o-o-l; school"

"Meadowlark capital M-e-a-d-o-w-l-a-r-k; capital M-e-a-d-o-w-l-a-r-k; capital M-e-a-d-o-w-l-a-r-k; Meadowlark"

Model how to write the new words and have the students write them.

fies
tried
families
Meadowlark
school

Focus on these five new words for two or three days. Help your students explain that school does not need a capital because it is not a specific school like Meadowlark. Have them name any other schools they know about and write these to show them that all school names begin with a capital letter. Spend two or three days reviewing the old words. Each day lead your students to cheer for five words but include some old words and some new words. Dictate a few sentences for your students to write that include word wall words, words and rhyming words from the first 100 words, and the names of your students.

Is Meadowlark your favorite school?
What do you do after school?
How many days are there until Thanksgiving?
Michael tried out for his favorite sport.

Continue to add five words each week, following these procedures for each group of words:

- Use new words in sentences to make sure your students have them in their oral vocabulary.
- For two days, focus only on the new words by leading your students to cheer for and write the new words.
- Add the specific names and general names in pairs and have your students explain why the specific names are capitalized and give other examples of specific teachers, cities, and streets.
- For three days, choose five words to cheer for that include some old words and some new words.
- Model sentences for your students to write that include new and old words.

● Review the First 50 Words

When you have 50 words on your wall, take a few weeks to review your word wall words and teach rhyming patterns and spelling changes. WORDO is a popular way to review key words. Make copies of a sheet with 25 squares. Have students choose 25 of the 50 word wall words and write them—one to a square. When your students have their WORDO sheets ready, call out words from the wall until someone has covered all the words on his or her card. Check to see that all the words the winner covered were called and they are all spelled correctly.

favorite	laugh	pretty	Chicago	I'll
sport	wasn't	swimming	build	great
many	until	were	sister	brother
Thanksgiving	under	off	pretty	place
because	around	animal	does	getting

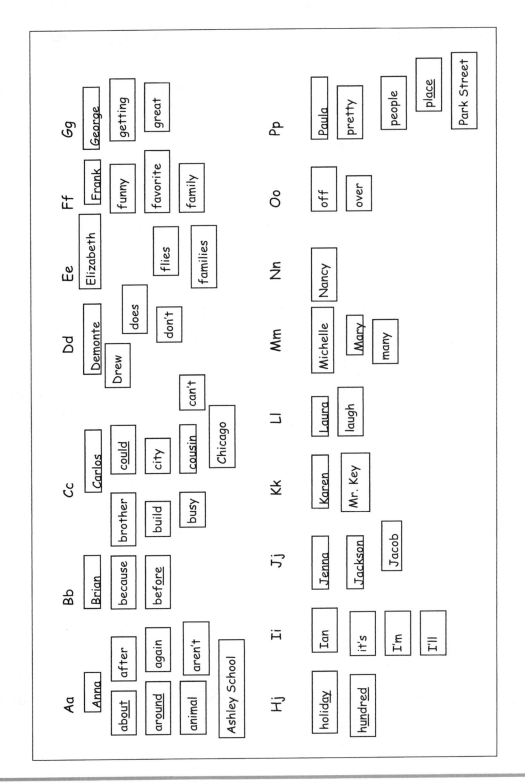

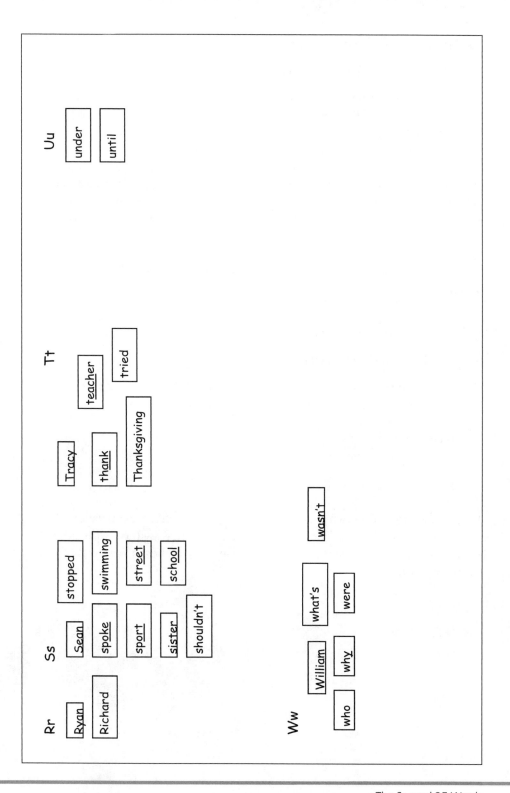

Rr

Ryan
Richard

Ss

Sean
spoke
sport
sister
shouldn't
stopped
swimming
street
school

Tt

Tracy
thank
Thanksgiving
teacher
tried

Uu

under
until

Ww

who
William
why
what's
were
wasn't

Teaching Your Students to Capitalize Specific Nouns

This set of words contains four common nouns and four specific nouns. After the children can spell these words, help them generalize about which words are capitalized. Draw students' attention to the words *holiday* and *Thanksgiving*. Ask them why *Thanksgiving* begins with a capital letter but *holiday* does not. Help them verbalize that Thanksgiving is a specific holiday. Do the same thing with the words *city* and *town, street* and *school,* and with whatever specific city or town, street and school names you have added to your word wall. Help them to notice that when we include the word *school* or *street* in the name (Ashley School; Park Street), that word also starts with a capital letter. Ask students to tell you the names of other specific holidays, towns, cities, streets, and schools and write these words in a list so that they can see that all these specific holidays and places begin with a capital letter.

Teaching Your Students the y to i Spelling Change

When your students have learned to spell *tried, flies,* and *families,* write these words on the board and write the words *try, fly,* and *family* next to them.

tries try
flies fly
families family

Discuss how in all three words, the *y* was changed to *i* before *es* or *ed* were added.

Give your students practice changing the *y* to *i* by having them write other words they know that end in *y* on a piece of paper. Write these same words on your board or chart.

dry
spy
cry
fry
city

Call out the following words and have the students write them next to the appropriate word, changing the *y* to an *i* before adding *es* or *ed*: *cried fried dries spies dried spied cities fries cries*.

dry	dries	dried
spy	spies	spied
cry	cried	cries
fry	fried	fries
city	cities	

● Teaching Your Students to Spell Rhyming Words

This set of words contains four new rhyming patterns: *ed, eet, ool,* and *ace*. To teach your students to use the words they know in order to spell other words, use the three-column chart format to help them choose the rhyming words. For each word, choose a word that ends the same from the first set of 100 words. Call out words and ask the children to decide which key word they rhyme with and write the word in the appropriate column.

street	at	about
sheet	flat	shout
feet	that	trout
greet	brat	spout
beet		scout
meet		

To make sure they understand that you want them to use these rhyming spelling patterns when they are writing, model how to write a sentence that uses a few of the rhyming words and some word wall words. Have your students write a sentence using at least two of the rhyming words.

My brother has flat feet.

school	all	will
stool	small	grill
pool	stall	chill
tool	wall	thrill
cool		still
carpool		

Do you come to school in a carpool?

place	price	grows
face	rice	rows
trace	mice	flows
race	twice	shows
brace	slice	
pace		

Carlton ran at a quick pace to win the race.

You can also use the WORDO game to help students practice rhyming words. Write 24 words that rhyme with word wall words on index cards and have students choose where to write them on the WORDO sheet. Shuffle and call the words. Be sure the words are spelled correctly when someone wins WORDO.

sunny	would	cookout	background	ignore
should	vanpool	heatstroke	Grace	space
greet	score	WORDO	tweet	whirlpool
ground	drool	dropout	scout	crank
feet	yank	hound	pound	preschool

Note: New words and patterns are **bold**; rhyming patterns are highlighted.

Sets 1 and 2	Words they should be able to spell
about	pout scout shout snout spout sprout trout blackout cookout dropout handout tryout
after	
again	
around	bound found ground hound mound pound round sound background aground
animal	
because	
before	bore chore core more score shore store tore wore ashore ignore restore outscore
brother	
build	
busy	
city	
could	would should
cousin	
does	

funny	bunny sunny
family	
favorite	
great	
holiday	
hundred	**bed fed Fred led Ned red shed shred sled sped Ted**
laugh	
many	
off	
over	
people	
place	**ace brace face grace Grace lace pace race space trace backspace**
pretty	
school	**cool drool fool pool spool stool tool wool carpool vanpool whirlpool preschool**
sister	
spoke	broke choke Coke joke poke smoke stroke woke awoke heatstroke sunstroke
sport	fort port short sort report deport import
street	**beet feet greet meet sheet sleet sweet tweet**
teacher	
thank	bank blank crank drank Frank plank prank rank sank spank tank yank outrank
Thanksgiving	
under	
until	
were	
who	
why	by shy why cry dry fry fly pry sky sly spy try standby rely deny

getting	batted batting chatted chatting patted patting betted betting petted petting setting hitting quitting spitting trotted trotting cutting shutting
swimming	crammed cramming rammed ramming slammed slamming dimmed dimming trimmed trimming
stopped	napped napping clapped clapping rapped, rapping, snapped snapping slapped slapping zapped zapping chipped chipping dipped dipping flipped flipping nipped ripped sipped sipping shipped shipping tipped tripped chopped chopping dropped dropping flopped flopping hopped hopping plopped plopping popped popping shopped shopping stopping topped topping
families	**cities**
flies	**cries dries fries pries spies**
tried	**cried dried fried pried spied**
teacher name	
school name	
street name	
city name	

You're the Expert!

I may be the expert on spelling but you are the expert on your kids! When deciding which words to include in all the lists, I tried to include only words that most young children would have in their listening vocabularies and that you could help them connect meaning for by putting the word in a sentence. I also used this criterion to decide which words to include that needed spelling changes. I included the words *cried, dried, fried, pried,* and *spied* because I thought most children would understand these words in sentences such as, "*Sean spied his favorite car under the couch and pried it out.*" I did not include other words such as *vied* or *shied* because I couldn't think of a sentence that would clue young children to their meaning. But, remember, you are the expert on your kids. Omit from all my lists words to which your students cannot connect meanings and add any you think they might know. Look at the lists throughout the chapter as starting points for customizing your own list of words.

The Third 25 Words

When all your students can spell the first 50 word wall words and rhyming words and most of your children can use the doubling and changing *y* to *i* rules correctly, you are ready to begin working with the third set. The third set of 25 words contains 7 common words that many students have difficulty spelling:

almost   also   always   once   really   surprise   tomorrow

Two key words are included to teach the spelling change that when a word ends in *e,* you drop the *e* before adding *ed* or *ing.*

writing   used

Nine of the most common contractions are also taught:

aren't   don't   can't   wasn't   shouldn't   what's   it's   I'll   I'm

Seven common compound words complete this set of 25 words:

into   outside   weekend   campfire   football   bedroom   birthday

The key words in this list will also allow you to teach five new spelling patterns: *end* (week**end**); *eek* (w**eek**end); *oom* (bedr**oom**); *amp* (c**amp**fire); *ire* (campf**ire**).

If You Teach Older Children

If you teach older children, you need to decide which, if any, of these words to include. Many older children misspell common illogically spelled words such as *almost* and *also* and contractions. They may not know that you drop the e when adding *ed* or *ing*. Dictate the following paragraph and have students write it.

I have **always** lik<u>ed</u> to hide. You *can't* tell where *I'm* hid<u>ing</u>. *I'll* **really surprise** you. You **also** *shouldn't* think of fak<u>ing</u> me out.

Seat your students so that they cannot see what anyone else is writing. Tell them that you want to assess their writing and they should do the best they can. Keep a reasonable pace that does not allow them to labor over the spelling of words. Assess their spelling needs by considering the three criteria this set of words is intended to teach.

- Look at the spelling of the bold words (**surprise, always, really, also**) to determine if your students know how to spell these illogically spelled common words.
- Look at the underlined words (<u>liked</u>, <u>hiding</u>, <u>faking</u>) to determine if they know the drop e spelling rule.
- Look at the italicized words (*can't, I'm, I'll, shouldn't*) to determine if they can spell common contractions.

If you determine that some of your children need any of these words, add whichever words they need—adding no more than five words each week. When you have added the words you determined they need and provided lots of practice with those words, dictate the paragraph to them again. If only a few of your students need any of these words, add those words to their personal word walls.

● Teaching the Words, Spelling Changes, and Contractions

Add these words gradually to your wall—no more than five each week. You may add them in any order, but it is probably best to add *used* and *writing* that are key words for the spelling change in the same week. *Also, almost,* and *always* should probably also be added in the same week.

almost	always	also	bedroom	birthday
campfire	football	into	once	outside
really	surprise	tomorrow	weekend	writing
used	aren't	can't	don't	I'll
I'm	it's	shouldn't	wasn't	what's

Use the procedures outlined for the first two sets to teach your students to spell these 25 words, the sounds for the common blends, and how to spell words that rhyme with the word wall words and begin with blends.

- Add words to the wall gradually, no more than five each week.
- On the day you add new words and the following day, lead your students to cheer three times for each new word and model the writing of each word.
- For two or three days each week, call out five words you want to review and lead your students to cheer for these words. Give the children lots of practice with the illogically spelled words.
- On review days, model how to write word wall words in sentences and include rhyming words they can spell based on the highlighted patterns.

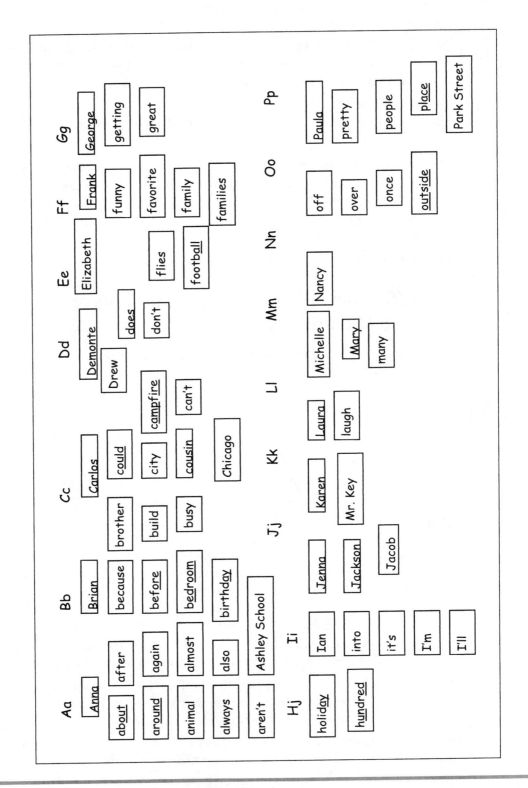

Aa

about · Anna
around · after
animal · again
always · almost
aren't · also
· Ashley School

Bb

Brian
because
before
bedroom
birthday

Cc

Carlos
brother · could
build · city
busy · campfire
· cousin
Chicago · can't

Dd

Demonte · does
Drew · don't

Ee

Elizabeth
flies
football

Ff

Frank
funny
favorite
family
families

Gg

George
getting
great

Hj

holiday
hundred

Ii

Ian
into
it's
I'm
I'll

Jj

Jenna
Jackson
Jacob

Kk

Karen
Mr. Key

Ll

Laura
laugh

Mm

Michelle
Mary
many · Nancy

Nn

Oo

off
over
once
outside

Pp

Paula
pretty
people
place
Park Street

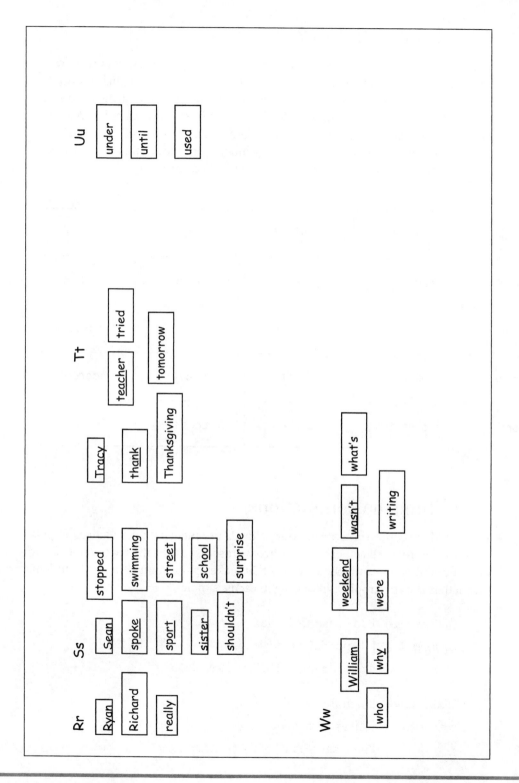

Rr

Ryan
Richard
really

Ss

Sean
spoke
sport
sister
shouldn't

stopped
swimming
street
school
surprise

Tt

Tracy
thank
Thanksgiving

teacher
tomorrow

tried

Uu

under
until
used

Ww

William
why
who

weekend
were

wasn't

what's
writing

● Review the First 75 Words

When you have 75 words on your wall, take a few weeks to review your word wall words and teach rhyming patterns and spelling changes. To create their WORDO sheet, have students choose 25 of the 75 word wall words and write them—one to a square. When your students have their WORDO sheets ready, call out words from the wall until someone has covered all the words on his or her card. The first person to cover the card completely is the winner. Check to see that all the words the winner covered were called and they are all spelled correctly.

outside	families	hundred	birthday	animal
always	campfire	people	used	weekend
surprise	writing	tomorrow	teacher	once
Thanksgiving	spoke	wasn't	really	bedroom
sport	street	could	cousin	favorite

● Teaching the Contractions

As you add the contractions, have your students use them in oral sentences. Repeat the sentences they tell you but use the two words rather than the contraction. Then write the contraction and the two words that make up the contraction. Ask students what letters the apostrophe is replacing in each example.

Child's sentence: I don't like anchovies.

Your sentence: I do not like anchovies.

don't do not "The ' replaces the o."

Child's sentence: I'm in third grade.

Your sentence: I am in third grade.

I'm I am "The ' replaces the a."

Child's sentence:	What's your name?
Your sentence:	What is your name?
	what's what is "The ' replaces the i."

Next, say some sentences that do not use the contractions and have your students tell you the sentence with the contraction. Write the contractions and ask them what letter the apostrophe replaces.

Your sentence:	You should not come to school if you have a fever.
Sentence with contraction:	You shouldn't come to school if you have a fever.
	should not shouldn't

Your sentence:	Paul was not here yesterday.
Sentence with contraction:	Paul wasn't here yesterday.
	was not wasn't

Your sentence:	I will see you at the game.
Sentence with contraction:	I'll see you at the game.
	I will I'll

When cheering the contractions, have your students gesture and make a clicking sound for the apostrophe.

● Teaching Your Students the Drop e Spelling Change

When your students have learned to spell *used* and *writing*, write these words on the board and write the words *use* and *write* next to them.

used	use
writing	write

Discuss how in these words, the *e* at the end was dropped before *ed* or *ing* were added.

Give your students practice with dropping the *e* by having them write other words they know that end in *e* on a piece of paper. Write these same words on your board or chart.

skate

hike

joke

slice

wire

wade

rake

Call out the following words and have them write them next to the appropriate word changing the *e* before adding *ing* or *ed: joking   waded   raking   slicing   sliced   hiked   wired   skated   skating   hiking   wiring   joked   wading   raked.*

skate	skated	skating
hike	hiked	hiking
joke	joking	joked
slice	slicing	sliced
wire	wired	wiring
wade	waded	wading
rake	raking	raked

● Teaching Your Students to Spell Rhyming Words

This set of words contains five new rhyming patterns: *amp, eek, end, ire,* and *oom.* To teach them to use the words they know in order to spell other words, use the three-column chart format to help them choose the rhyming words. Use previously taught words so that the three words have the same ending sound. Call out words and have your students decide which key word they rhyme with and write the word in the appropriate column.

week	spoke	look
seek	broke	brook
cheek	choke	shook
creek	poke	crook
peek	woke	hook

To make sure they understand that you want them to use these rhyming spelling patterns when they are writing, model how to write a sentence that uses a few of the rhyming words and some word wall words. Have your students write a sentence using at least two of the rhyming words.

I like to wade in the brook and the creek.

You can also use the WORDO game to help students practice rhyming words. Write 24 words that rhyme with word wall words on index cards and have students choose where to write them on the WORDO sheet. Shuffle and call the words. Be sure the words are spelled correctly when someone wins WORDO.

groom	feet	greet	stamp	space
shred	pool	creek	Grace	broom
cramp	Fred	WORDO	weekend	bookroom
bloom	backfire	playroom	spend	champ
hire	peek	tire	defend	bend

Note: New words and patterns are **bold**; rhyming patterns are highlighted.

Sets 1, 2, and 3	Words they should be able to spell
about	pout scout shout snout spout sprout trout blackout cookout dropout handout tryout
after	
again	
around	bound found ground hound mound pound round sound background aground
almost	
also	
always	
animal	
because	
bedroom	boom bloom broom doom gloom groom room zoom backroom ballroom coatroom playroom newsroom
before	bore chore core more score shore store tore wore ashore ignore restore outscore
birthday	
brother	
build	
busy	
campfire	camp champ clamp cramp damp lamp ramp stamp tramp streetlamp fire hire tire wire backfire umpire inspire retire require
city	
could	would should
cousin	
does	
funny	bunny sunny

family	
favorite	
football	
great	
holiday	
hundred	bed fed Fred led Ned red shed shred sled sped Ted
into	
laugh	
many	
off	
once	
outside	
over	
people	
place	ace brace face grace Grace lace pace race space trace backspace
pretty	
really	
school	cool drool fool pool spool stool tool wool carpool vanpool whirlpool preschool
sister	
spoke	broke choke Coke joke poke smoke stroke woke awoke heatstroke sunstroke
sport	fort port short sort report deport import
street	beet feet greet meet sheet sleet sweet tweet
surprise	
teacher	
thank	bank blank crank drank Frank plank prank rank sank spank tank yank outrank
Thanksgiving	

tomorrow	
under	
until	
weekend	**bend blend end lend mend send spend tend trend defend depend** **cheek creek geek peek seek sleek week**
were	
who	
why	by shy why cry dry fry fly pry sky sly spy try standby rely deny
aren't	**weren't**
can't	
don't	**won't**
shouldn't	**couldn't wouldn't**
wasn't	**doesn't isn't**
I'll	**you'll we'll he'll she'll they'll**
I'm	
it's	**he's she's that's there's here's**
what's	
getting	batted batting chatted chatting patted patting betted betting petted petting setting hitting quitting spitting trotted trotting cutting shutting
swimming	crammed cramming rammed ramming slammed slamming dimmed dimming trimmed trimming
stopped	napped napping clapped clapping rapped, rapping, snapped snapping slapped slapping zapped zapping chipped chipping dipped dipping flipped flipping nipped ripped sipped sipping shipped shipping tipped tripped chopped chopping dropped dropping flopped flopping hopped hopping plopped plopping popped popping shopped shopping stopping topped topping
families	cities
flies	cries dries fries pries spies

tried	cried dried fried pried spied
used	**baked faked raked graded traded waded rated skated iced sliced biked hiked fired hired wired choked joked poked smoked**
writing	**baking faking making raking shaking taking waking grading trading wading skating icing slicing riding hiding sliding biking hiking firing hiring wiring choking joking poking smoking using**
teacher name	
school name	
street name	
city name	

The Final 25 Words

When all your students can spell the first 75 word wall words and rhyming words and most of the children can use the doubling, dropping *e*, and changing *y* to *i* rules correctly, you are ready to begin working with the final set. This set of 25 words contains two season words and four more compound words

summer   winter   without   myself   skateboard   homework

Four key words are included to teach the spelling change that when a word ends in *o, ss, sh,* or *ch,* you need to add an *es* to spell words that end with the *s* ending.

goes   glasses   catches   wishes

Two days of the week are included so that you can teach your students that we capitalize the names of the days of the week:

Monday   Saturday

This set also includes the most common homophones:

To, too, two; there, their, they're; no, know; right, write; wear, where, we're

The key words in this list can be used to teach three new spelling patterns: *ass* (glasses); *atch* (catches); and *ish* (wishes).

If You Teach Older Children

If you teach older children, you need to decide which, if any, of these words to include. Many older children misspell homophones and do not know that you add *es* to words that end in *sh, ch, ss,* or *o.* Some of your students may not know that specific days of the week need capital letters. To determine if your students need any of these words on the wall, dictate the following paragraph to them and have them write the paragraph without any help from you.

> On *Friday* in winter, **there** are **two** things I do. I **write to** Fay. **We're** friends. I also call Mick **to** meet me on *Sunday.* He go<u>es</u> **right where** I like **to** play. He dash<u>es</u> **there** on his bike.

Seat your students so that they cannot see what anyone else is writing. Tell them that you want to assess their writing and they should do the best they can. Keep a reasonable pace that does not allow them to labor over the spelling of words. Assess their spelling needs by considering the three criteria this set of words is intended to teach.

- Look at the spelling of the bold words (**to, two, write, right, there, their, we're, where**) to determine if your students know how to spell these common homophones.
- Look at the underlined words (go<u>es</u>, dash<u>es</u>) to determine if they know to add *es* to words that end in *ss, sh,* or *ch.*
- Look at the first letter of the italicized words (*Friday, Sunday*) to determine if they know that you capitalize specific days of the week.

If you determine that your students need any of these words, add whichever words they need—adding no more than five words each week. If only a few of your students need any of these words, add those words to their personal word walls.

● Teaching the Words, Spelling Changes, and Homophones

Add these words gradually to your wall—no more than five each week. You can add them in any order, but it is probably best to add *goes, glasses, wishes,* and *catches* that are key words for the spelling change in the same week. Homophones should be added in the same week and a clue attached to all but one of them so that your students can learn their meanings.

summer winter without myself skateboard homework Monday Saturday goes glasses catches wishes

to, too, two; there, their, they're; no, know; right, write; wear, where, we're

Use the procedures outlined for the first two sets to teach your students to spell these 25 words.

- Add words to the wall gradually, no more than five each week.
- On the day you add new words and the following day, lead your student to cheer three times for each new word and model the writing of each word.
- Add sets of homophones in the same week, along with clues to the meaning of all but one of them.
- Point out that Monday and Saturday are specific days and that all seven days of the week begin with capital letters.
- For two days each week, call out five words you want to review and lead your students to cheer for these words. Give your students lots of practice with the illogically spelled words.
- Review old and new words for three days. On review days, model how to write word wall words in sentences and include rhyming words they can spell based on the highlighted patterns.
- When you have all 25 words on your wall, take a few days to consolidate your word wall words by letting your students play a few rounds of WORDO. Make copies of a sheet with 9 squares. Write the 25 new words on index cards—one to a card. Have your students choose 9 of the 25 words and write them—one to a square. When your students have their WORDO sheets ready, shuffle your cards and call out words until someone has covered all the words on their card. The first person to cover the card completely is the winner and should shout, "WORDO." Check to see that all the words the winner covered were called and they are all spelled correctly on his or her sheet. If you have time, have the children clear their cards and play another round.

summer	two	catches
Monday	glasses	too
right	homework	skateboard

● Teaching the Homophones

Add the sets of homophones in the same week. Put a clue on all but one of them so that your students will learn which word has which meaning. For *two*, *too* and *to*, attach a card with the number 2 next to *two*. Since *too* has two meanings, attach two cards showing both meanings. When you add *there, their,* and *they're,* underline the *here* in *there* and help your students see that the word *there* is the opposite of the word here. Attach a card with the words *they are* next to *they're*. For *wear, where,* and *we're,* attach a card with question marks to *where*. A card with the words *we are* can be attached to the word *we're*. A picture of a pencil (or a real pencil) can be attached next to the word *write* to distinguish it from *right*. Attach a card with the word *yes* next to *no* to make the meanings of *no* and *know* clear.

● Teaching Your Students the es Spelling Change

When your students have learned to spell *goes, glasses, catches,* and *wishes,* write these words on the board and write the words *go, glass, catch,* and *wish* next to them.

goes	go
glasses	glass
catches	catch
wishes	wish

Help the children to notice that when words end in *o, ss, ch,* or *sh* they need to add *es* instead of just *s*. Give your students practice with adding *es* by writing some words that add just the *s* and some that need *es*. Write these same words on your board or chart.

pass

patch

match

class

pitch

kiss

bath

chill

miss

dish

cash

mash

spill

smash

path

rush

Call out the following words and have the children write them next to the appropriate word, adding *s* or *es* as needed: passes patches matches classes pitches kisses baths chills misses dishes cashes mashes spills smashes paths rushes.

pass	passes
patch	patches
match	matches
class	classes
pitch	pitches
kiss	kisses
bath	baths
chill	chills
miss	misses
dish	dishes
cash	cashes
mash	mashes
spill	spills
smash	smashes
path	paths
rush	rushes

Ask the children to write a sentence using at least two of the words that add *es*.

The pitcher pitches the ball but the batter misses it.

Teaching Your Students to Spell Rhyming Words

This set of words contains three new rhyming patterns, *ass, atch,* and *ish.* To teach your students to use the words they know in order to spell other words, use the three-column chart format to help them choose the rhyming words. Call out words and have your students decide which key word they rhyme with and write the word in the appropriate column.

catch	wish	grass
snatch	dish	class
patch	fish	glass
match	goldfish	pass
rematch	catfish	overpass

To make sure they understand that you want them to use these rhyming spelling patterns when they are writing, model how to write a sentence that uses a few of the rhyming words and some word wall words. Have your students write a sentence using at least two of the rhyming words.

I like to eat catfish but I don't eat goldfish.

You can also use the WORDO game to help students practice rhyming words. Write 24 words that rhyme with word wall words on index cards and have students choose where to write them on the WORDO sheet. Shuffle and call the words. Be sure the words are spelled correctly when someone wins WORDO.

groom	feet	greet	stamp	space
shred	pool	creek	Grace	broom
cramp	Fred	**WORDO**	weekend	bookroom
bloom	backfire	playroom	spend	champ
hire	peek	tire	defend	bend

Note: New words and patterns are **bold**; rhyming patterns are highlighted.

Sets 1, 2, 3, and 4	Words they should be able to spell
about	pout scout shout snout spout sprout trout blackout cookout dropout handout tryout
after	
again	
around	bound found ground hound mound pound round sound background aground
almost	
also	
always	
animal	
because	
bedroom	boom bloom broom doom gloom groom room zoom backroom ballroom coatroom playroom newsroom
before	bore chore core more score shore store tore wore ashore ignore restore outscore
birthday	
brother	

build	
busy	
campfire	camp champ clamp cramp damp lamp ramp stamp tramp streetlamp fire hire tire wire backfire umpire inspire retire require
city	
could	would should
cousin	
does	
funny	bunny sunny
family	
favorite	
football	
great	
holiday	
homework	
hundred	bed fed Fred led Ned red shed shred sled sped Ted
into	
laugh	
many	
Monday	
myself	himself herself yourself
off	
once	
outside	
people	
place	ace brace face grace Grace lace pace race space trace backspace
pretty	

really	
Saturday	
school	cool drool fool pool spool stool tool wool carpool vanpool whirlpool preschool
sister	
skateboard	
spoke	broke choke Coke joke poke smoke stroke woke awoke heatstroke sunstroke
sport	fort port short sort report deport import
street	beet feet greet meet sheet sleet sweet tweet
summer	
surprise	
teacher	
thank	bank blank crank drank Frank plank prank rank sank spank tank yank outrank
Thanksgiving	
tomorrow	
over	
under	
until	
weekend	bend blend end lend mend send spend tend trend defend depend cheek creek geek peek seek sleek week
were	
winter	
without	
who	
why	by shy why cry dry fry fly pry sky sly spy try standby rely deny
aren't	weren't
can't	

don't	won't
shouldn't	couldn't wouldn't
wasn't	didn't doesn't isn't
I'll	you'll we'll he'll she'll they'll
I'm	
it's	he's she's that's there's here's
what's	
to	
too	
two	
there	
their	
they're	
wear	
where	
we're	
no	
know	
right	
write	
goes	
glasses	**bass brass class (es) grass mass pass (es) overpass underpass**
catches	**batch (es) hatch (es) match (es) patch (es) snatch (es) rematch**
wishes	**dish (es) fish squish (es) swish (es) goldfish blackfish redfish catfish finish (es) vanish (es) punish (es)**
getting	batted batting chatted chatting patted patting betted betting petted petting setting hitting quitting spitting trotted trotting cutting shutting

swimming	crammed cramming rammed ramming slammed slamming dimmed dimming trimmed trimming
stopped	napped napping clapped clapping rapped, rapping, snapped snapping slapped slapping zapped zapping chipped chipping dipped dipping flipped flipping nipped ripped sipped sipping shipped shipping tipped tripped chopped chopping dropped dropping flopped flopping hopped hopping plopped plopping popped popping shopped shopping stopping topped topping
families	cities
flies	cries dries fries pries spies
tried	cried dried fried pried spied
used	baked faked raked graded traded waded rated skated iced sliced biked hiked fired hired wired choked joked poked smoked
writing	baking faking making raking shaking taking waking grading trading wading skating icing slicing riding hiding sliding biking hiking firing hiring wiring choking joking poking smoking using
teacher name	
school name	
street name	
city name	

Review, Consolidate, Celebrate!

When your students can spell the 100 key words in this chapter, they should be able to spell many words based on the rhyming patterns and spelling changes that these words represent. In addition, they should be automatically capitalizing the first letter of specific nouns. Take as much time as you can in the final weeks of school to review the words, help them consolidate their spelling strategies, and celebrate their spelling prowess!

You can use the WORDO game format to review the 100 words, the spelling changes, and the rhyming patterns.

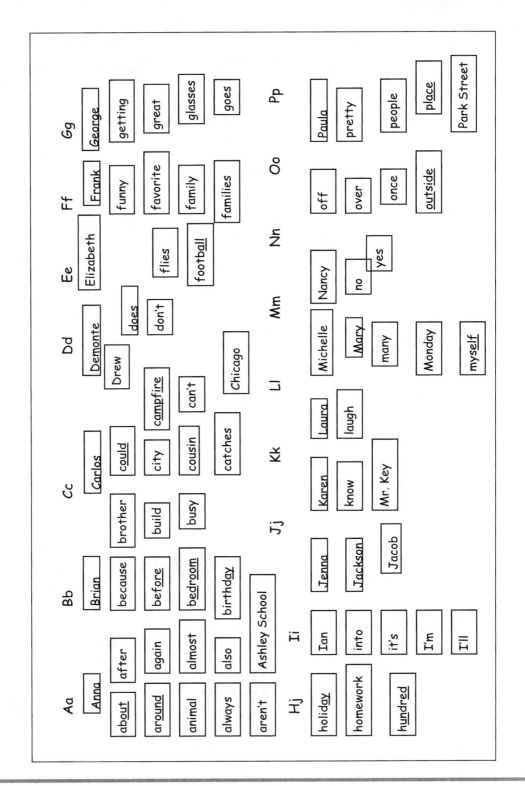

Aa
Anna
about
after
around
again
animal
almost
always
also
aren't
Ashley School

Bb
Brian
because
before
bedroom
birthday

Cc
Carlos
brother
could
build
city
campfire
busy
cousin
can't
catches
Chicago

Dd
Demonte
Drew
does
don't

Ee
Elizabeth
flies
football

Ff
Frank
funny
favorite
family
families

Gg
George
getting
great
glasses
goes

Hj
holiday
homework
hundred

Ii
Ian
into
it's
I'm
I'll

Jj
Jenna
Jackson
Jacob

Kk
Karen
know
Mr. Key
Laura
laugh

Ll

Mm
Michelle
Mary
many
Monday
myself
Nancy
no
yes

Nn

Oo
off
over
once
outside

Pp
Paula
pretty
people
place
Park Street

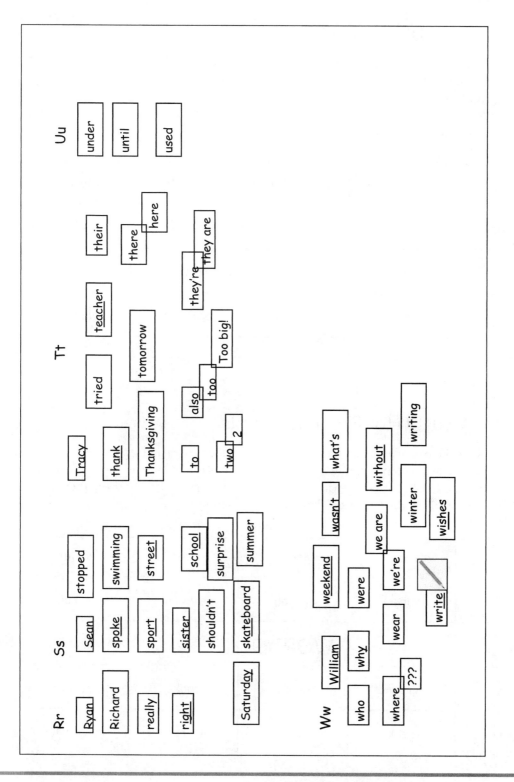

Rr
Ryan
Richard
really
right

Ss
Sean
spoke
sport
sister
shouldn't
Saturday
stopped
swimming
street
school
surprise
skateboard
summer

Tt
Tracy
thank
Thanksgiving
tried
tomorrow
also
too
to
two 2
teacher
Too big!
their
there here
they're they are

Uu
under
until
used

Ww
William
who
why
where ???
weekend
were
wear
wasn't
we are
we're
write
what's
without
winter
wishes
writing

● WORDO for Key Words

Have students choose 25 of the 100 key words and write them in the squares. Shuffle a deck of 100 index cards with key words written on them and call out words until someone wins. Check to be sure the winner has only covered words that have been called and that the words are spelled correctly. You can play for rows, columns, diagonals, or a full card.

around	campfire	Monday	myself	football
Saturday	without	shouldn't	glasses	swimming
wasn't	catches	summer	families	winter
right	write	they're	surprise	laugh
weekend	people	favorite	cousin	animal

● WORDO for Rhyming Words

Write 30 to 40 words that can be spelled using the new rhyming patterns on index cards. Have students choose 24 to write on their WORDO sheets. Shuffle and call out words. Check that the winners have the words spelled correctly and then have everyone clear their sheets and play another round.

score	rematch	umpire	ground	shout
squish	champ	carpool	newsroom	cookout
blend	grass	WORDO	sled	groom
deny	aground	bunny	choke	prank
depend	geek	spy	underpass	sunstroke

● WORDO for Spelling Changes

Write 30 to 40 words with spelling changes on index cards. Have students choose 24 of these words and write them in the squares. Shuffle the deck and call out words until someone wins. Check to be sure the winner has only covered words that have been called and that the words are spelled correctly. You can play for rows, columns, diagonals or a full card.

batted	punishes	sliced	setting	shopped
passes	spies	quitting	cities	finishes
hatches	hiding	WORDO	topping	trimmed
vanishes	flopped	slammed	snatches	fried
tripped	skated	joked	biking	baking

● Be a Mind Reader

Be a Mind Reader is another game you can use to review word wall words. In this game, you think of a word on the wall and then give five clues to that word. Choose a word and write it on a scrap of paper but do not let the students see what word you have written. Tell each student to number a piece of paper from 1 to 5. Explain that you are going to see who can read your mind and figure out which of the words on the wall you are thinking of and have written on your paper. Tell them you will give them five clues. By the fifth clue, everyone should guess your word, but if they read your mind they might get it before the fifth clue. Since you now have 100 words on your wall and your students' names, give a first clue which limits the words to 6 or 7 alphabet letters. Tell your students to write next to number 1 the word they think it might be. Each succeeding clue should narrow down what it can be until by clue 5 there is only one possible word. As you give clues, students write the word they believe it is next to each number. If succeeding clues confirm the word a student has written next to one number, the student writes that word again by the next number. If succeeding clues eliminate the word, students choose a new word that fits all the clues.

After clue 5, show students the word you wrote on your scrap paper and say, "I know you all have the word next to number 5 but who has it next to number 4?

3? 2? 1?" All students who guessed the word on line 1 are the winners. If no one guessed it on line 1, the winners are everyone who guessed it on line 2. In the unlikely event that no one guessed it on line 1 or 2, the winners are everyone who guessed it on line 3. Once you have your winners, check their papers to make sure the word is spelled correctly every time. If someone has not spelled the word correctly, he or she does not win! Here are some examples to get you started.

1. It's a word wall word that starts with *a, b, c, d, e,* or *f.*
2. It has 6 letters.
3. It begins with *c.*
4. It does not have an *s.*
5. A dog, bear, ant, lizard, and fish are all one of these.

1. It's a word wall word that starts with *t, u, v, w, x, y,* or *z.*
2. It has 6 or more letters.
3. It begins with *t.*
4. It is not a person.
5. It is a holiday we celebrate on the fourth Thursday in November.

1. It's a word wall word that starts with *g, h, i, j, k, l,* or *m.*
2. It does not have an *i.*
3. It has 6 or more letters.
4. It is a compound word.
5. You have to do this every night except Fridays!

1. It's a word wall word that starts with *n, o, p, q, r , s,* or *t.*
2. It has 6 letters.
3. It does not begin with *s.*
4. It ends with *y.*
5. It begins with *r.*

● Ruler Tap

Ruler Tap is a simple activity but children love it and it does help them review the words. Begin the game by saying a word wall word and tapping the ruler for several of the letters (without saying them). When you stop tapping, call on a student to finish spelling the word out loud. If that student correctly finishes spelling the word, give the ruler to that student and let him or her call out a word and tap some of the letters. That student calls on another student and if that student correctly finishes spelling the word, he or she gets the ruler and the game continues!

● Rhyme Riddles

Children enjoy all kinds of riddles. Make up some riddles in which the answer rhymes with a key word. Tell your students to work in partners or trios to solve the riddles. After they understand how rhyme riddles work, let them work together to write some for their classmates to solve. Give them a list of the key words with rhyming patterns from the first 200 words to use as key words:

Key Words for Rhyming Patterns from First 200 Words				
all	am	and	around	at
bedroom	before	best	big	black
boy	bright	but	camp	campfire
can	clown	coat	crash	did
drink	each	eat	end	flag
girl	good	grow	had	how
in	it	jump	kind	like
look	made	make	my	not
old	out	pet	place	play
price	quick	ride	run	saw
school	see	skate	sleep	smart
snap	spell	spoke	sport	stop
street	swim	talk	thank	thing
train	up	went	when	will

Here are a few examples:

I am what is left when a tree is cut down. I rhyme with jump. What am I?

I am the highest card in the deck. I rhyme with place. What am I?

I am what you use to cook hot dogs outside. I rhyme with will. What am I?

I am the opposite of tall. I rhyme with sport. What am I?

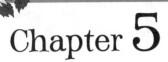

Chapter 5

Developing a Visual Checking Sense

This chapter contains lists and activities for teaching the third 100 most important words all elementary students need to be able to spell.

Like the first and second 100 words, the words are divided into 4 sets of 25 each. If you teach third or fourth grade, these 100 words are probably the ones most appropriate for your grade. Regardless of what grade level you teach, the activities in this chapter assume that your students can spell the 200 words from the previous chapter and can use rhyming patterns to spell hundreds of other words. Activities in this chapter also assume that your students can use the spelling changes needed when endings are added to some words and can spell the most common contractions and homophones. Here are the second 100 words from the previous chapter. New spelling patterns are highlighted. Key words for spelling changes are italicized. Specific names that need capital letters are bold. If your students cannot spell these words and words with these rhyming and spelling change patterns, cycle back through Chapter 4.

The Second 100 Words				
about	after	again	almost	also
always	animal	aren't	around	because
bedroom	before	birthday	brother	build
busy	campfire	can't	catches	city
could	cousin	does	don't	*families*
family	favorite	*flies*	football	funny
getting	*glasses*	*goes*	great	holiday
homework	hundred	I'll	I'm	into
it's	know	laugh	many	**Monday**
myself	no	off	once	outside
over	people	place	pretty	really
right	**Saturday**	school	shouldn't	sister
skateboard	spoke	sport	*stopped*	street
summer	surprise	*swimming*	teacher	thank
Thanksgiving	their	there	they're	to
tomorrow	too	*tried*	two	under
until	*used*	wasn't	we're	wear
weekend	were	what's	where	who
why	winter	*wishes*	without	write
writing	**teacher name**	**school name**	**street name**	**city/town name**

If your students can spell common illogically spelled words, spell words based on rhyming patterns, know the spelling changes required by some words when endings are added, and understand that specific names for people, places, holidays, and other specific words begin with capital letters, they are well on their way to becoming excellent spellers. There is one more component of spelling that all good spellers need to master. All good spellers have a visual checking sense. Have you ever written a word and heard a little voice in your head announce, "That doesn't look right!" Have you ever been asked by someone to spell a word and responded, "Wait a minute. I have to write it!" If you have experienced either of these common scenarios, you know that in addition to following a known pattern, words have to "look right." As part of your spelling repertoire, you have a visual checking sense.

Except for the illogically spelled common words, words that rhyme are usually spelled with the same ending letters but some rhymes have two common spelling patterns. The rhyming part of *white* and *night* can be spelled i-t-e or i-g-h-t. The rhyming part of *year* and *cheer* can be spelled e-a-r and e-e-r. A few rhyming patterns have three common spelling patterns. *Phone, moan,* and *own* all rhyme and are spelled with the patterns o-n-e, o-a-n, and o-w-n.

Many of the homophones are words that are commonly spelled two different ways.

He was **weak** for a **week** after the surgery.

We **rode** our bikes down the country **road**.

The **bear** climbed the **bare**, snow covered tree.

This third group of 100 words contains more common illogically spelled words, reviews spelling changes by teaching some words that end with the suffixes *er, est, er* (person), and *en* and reviews the principle of capitalizing specific names by including key words for states, countries, and months. The most important goal for the lessons in this chapter, however, is to help all your students develop a visual checking sense. To accomplish this goal, this chapter contains more common homophones and many *What Looks Right?* lessons.

Do Your Older Students Have a Visual Checking Sense?

Do your older students have a visual checking sense? Do they spell by pattern but often use the wrong pattern? To determine if your students can spell some common illogically spelled words and have a visual checking sense, dictate this paragraph to them.

I went to a **restaurant** for a **special** meal with my **neighbor**. We both **thought** it was **terrible**. The wheat bread was stale. The prune soup tasted like glue. We were afraid to take **another** bite.

Before dictating the paragraph to your students, be sure they are seated where they can't see each other's papers. Tell them you want to see what writing skills they need to work on and they should just do the best they can. Do not tell them you are assessing their spelling. If they ask you how to spell a word, simply tell them to "do the best you can." Keep a reasonable pace in your dictation—giving them enough time to get the words down but not enough to labor over the spelling of each word. Remember, you are trying to get a snapshot of their spelling proficiency while writing so that you can determine which words need to be a part of your word wall and spelling instruction.

- Look at the spelling of the bold words (**restaurant, special, neighbor, terrible, thought, another**) to determine if any of these common words are misspelled by any of your students. The bold words are often misspelled by older children.

- Look at the spelling of the underlined words (m<u>ea</u>l, wh<u>ea</u>t, br<u>ea</u>d, st<u>a</u>le, pr<u>u</u>ne, gl<u>ue</u>, afr<u>aid</u>, b<u>ite</u>) to determine if your students have a visual checking sense. If students spell some of these words with the other possible pattern (m<u>ee</u>l, wh<u>ee</u>t, br<u>e</u>d, st<u>ai</u>l, pr<u>oo</u>n, gl<u>ew</u>, afr<u>ade</u>, b<u>ight</u>), they probably haven't developed a visual checking sense. The *What Looks Right?* lessons in this chapter will help them develop that sense.

Teaching the First 25 Words and a Visual Checking Sense

The first set of 25 words includes some illogically spelled common words, words that rhyme but have different spelling patterns, some common homophones, and the names of three months that are key words for learning that month names begin with capital letters.

another	believe	enough	minute	month
often	trouble	terrible	whale	trail
vote	float	tonight	white	soon
true	new	knew	hole	whole
one	won	December	February	June

Add these words gradually to your wall—no more than five each week. You can choose the order but add the homophone pairs in the same week. Add clues to one of the homophones so your students can remember which word has which meaning.

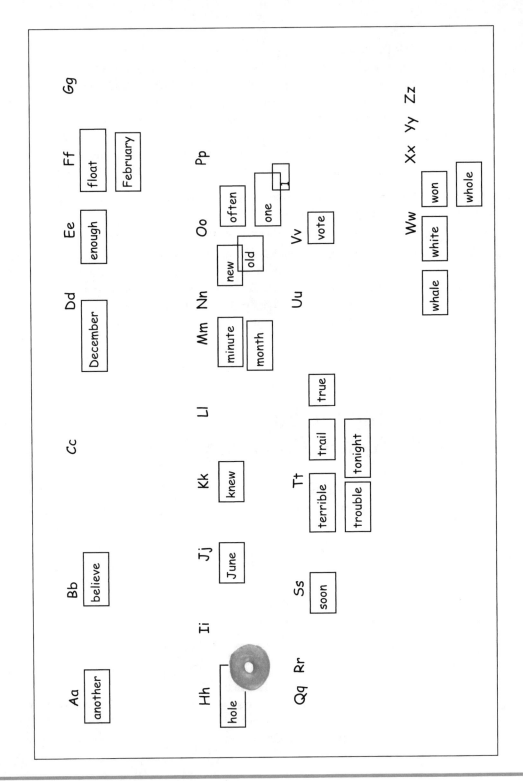

Aa another
Bb believe
Cc
Dd December
Ee enough
Ff float   February
Gg

Hh hole
Ii
Jj June
Kk knew
Ll
Mm minute   month
Nn
Oo new   old
Pp often   one
Qq Rr
Ss soon
Tt terrible   trail   true   trouble   tonight
Uu
Vv vote
Ww whale   white   won   whole
Xx Yy Zz

On the day you add words, have your students use these words in oral sentences to make sure they can associate meaning with the words. Have them create several sentences that show the meanings of the homophones. Get your students out of their seats and lead them to cheer for the five words—three times each word. Have them say the word they are cheering at the beginning and end.

"another a-n-o-t-h-e-r; a-n-o-t-h-e-r; a-n-o-t-h-e-r; another"

"believe b-e-l-i-e-v-e; b-e-l-i-e-v-e; b-e-l-i-e-v-e; believe"

"terrible t-e-r-r-i-b-l-e; t-e-r-r-i-b-l-e; t-e-r-r-i-b-l-e; terrible"

"new n-e-w; n-e-w; n-e-w; new"

"knew k-n-e-w; k-n-e-w; k-n-e-w; knew"

Next, have them write the words as you model correct letter formation.

another
believe
terrible
new
knew

For the next several days, continue to lead your students to cheer for and write these words. When they have written the words in a list for two or three days, have them write sentences with the words using at least two of the word wall words in each sentence.

Andy knew he was getting a new bike for his birthday.
No one could believe we were the new champs.
Yesterday we got another new student in our class.
Everyone knew something terrible was going to happen.

When all your students can spell these five words quickly and automatically, add five more words. Have students use the words in oral sentences. Lead your students to cheer the new words—three times each:

"enough e-n-o-u-g-h; e-n-o-u-g-h; e-n-o-u-g-h; enough"

"whale w-h-a-l-e; w-h-a-l-e; w-h-a-l-e; whale"

"trail t-r-a-i-l; t-r-a-i-l; t-r-a-i-l; trail"

"one o-n-e; o-n-e; o-n-e; one"

"won w-o-n; w-o-n; w-o-n; won"

Model for them how to write the new words and have them write them.

enough

whale

trail

one

won

Focus on these five new words for two days. Then spend three days reviewing the old words. Each day lead your students to cheer for five words but include some old words and some new words. Have your students write a few sentences, each of which contains at least two of the words.

Our team won the game by one point.

We got another pizza because one was not enough.

I could not believe we played such a terrible game and still won.

When all your students can spell these five words quickly and automatically, add five more words. Have students use the words in oral sentences. Lead your students to cheer the new words—three times each:

"month m-o-n-t-h; m-o-n-t-h; m-o-n-t-h; month"

"June capital J-u-n-e; capital J-u-n-e; capital J-u-n-e; June"

"December capital D-e-c-e-m-b-e-r; capital D-e-c-e-m-b-e-r; capital D-e-c-e-m-b-e-r; December"

"February capital F-e-b-r-u-a-r-y; capital F-e-b-r-u-a-r-y; capital F-e-b-r-u-a-r-y; February"

soon s-o-o-n; s-o-o-n; s-o-o-n; soon"

Model how to write the new words and have the students write them.

month

June

February

December

soon

Focus on these five new words for two days. Then spend three days reviewing the old words. Each day lead your students to cheer for five words but include some old words and some new words. Have your students write a few sentences, each of which contains at least two of the words.

December is my favorite month.
I can't believe June is almost here.
The city is building a new bike trail.

Spelling Skills Help Only if the Students Use Them When They Write!

The only reason your students need to learn how to spell words is to enable them to write fluently and well. If they learn to spell words during your spelling practice but do not spell them correctly when writing, your spelling practice is wasted. Provide weekly practice spelling the word wall words as they write a few sentences. When they are writing throughout the day, remind them to use the word wall and hold them accountable for spelling word wall words correctly in everything they write.

Continue to add five words each week following these procedures for each group of words.

- Have students put new words in sentences to make sure they have the correct meaning in their oral vocabulary. Have students make several sentences with the homophones.

- Add the word *month* and the specific month names and point out that December, February, and June are specific months and that all the names of the months begin with capital letters.

- For two days, focus only on the new words by leading your students to cheer for and write the new words.

- For three days, choose five words to cheer for including some old words and some new words.

- Have students write a few sentences and include at least two word wall words in each.

When you have all 25 words on your wall, take a few days to consolidate your word wall words by letting your students play a few rounds of WORDO. Make copies of a sheet with 9 squares. Have your children choose 9 of the 25 words and write them—one to a square. Meanwhile, make yourself a deck of calling cards by writing the 25 words on index cards—one to a card. When your students have their WORDO sheets ready, shuffle your cards and call out words until someone has covered all the words on his or her card. The first person to cover the card completely is the winner and should shout, "WORDO." Check to see that all the words the winner covered were called and they are all spelled correctly on his or her sheet. If you have time, have the students clear their cards and play another round. Using Cheerios or some other nutritious cereal to cover the words makes for quick clean-up and a nutritious snack!

December	tonight	float
month	whole	hole
terrible	trouble	won

● Teaching the Homophones

Add the sets of homophones in the same week. Put a clue on all but one of them so your students will learn which word has which meaning. For *new* and *knew*, attach a card with the word *old* next to *new* and explain, "This is the *new* that is the opposite of *old*." Attach a card with the number *1* next to *one*. For *hole* and *whole*, attach a card with a picture of a hole next to *hole*.

● Developing a Visual Checking Sense with What Looks Right?

What Looks Right? is an activity to help your students develop a visual checking sense and to teach them how to use the dictionary to check the spelling of a word. To begin a *What Looks Right?* lesson, create two columns headed by two words that rhyme and have different spelling patterns. Have your students write the same words in columns on their papers.

whale   trail

Have your students pronounce and spell the words and lead them to realize that the words rhyme but have a different spelling pattern. Highlight or underline the spelling pattern in *whale* and *trail* and have them do the same on their papers. Tell them that there are many words that rhyme with *whale* and *trail* and that you can't tell just by saying the words which spelling patterns these words will have. Next, say a word that rhymes with *whale* and *trail* and write it both ways, saying, "If the word is spelled like *whale*, it will be j-a-l-e. If it is spelled like *trail*, it will be j-a-i-l." Write these two possible spellings under the appropriate word.

whale	trail
jale	jail

Tell your students to decide which one "looks right" to them and to write **only the one** they think is correct. When the students have decided which one looks right and written this word in the correct column, ask your students to find the word in the dictionary to "prove they are right." Don't wait for everyone to find the correct spelling. As soon as anyone has found it, ask all your students to turn to that page and verify the correct spelling. If any of your students guessed wrong, have them erase the incorrect spelling and write the correct spelling. Cross out the spelling you wrote that is not correct and continue with another example.

For the first examples, choose common words that you think most of your students will instantly recognize which is the correct spelling. As you write each word, explain your thinking. "If it is spelled like *whale*, it will be n-a-l-e, but if it is spelled like *trail*, it will be n-a-i-l."

whale	trail
~~jale~~	jail
nale	nail

After you have written the word both ways, have your students choose the one they think is correct and write only that one. When they have made their choice, tell them to find the word in the dictionary to prove they were correct and then fix any incorrect spellings. Cross out your incorrect spelling.

whale	trail
~~jale~~	jail
~~nale~~	nail

Continue to add words and have your students guess and then check. As the lesson goes on, they should get quicker at finding the words in the dictionary.

whale	trail
~~jale~~	jail
~~nale~~	nail
scale	~~scail~~
~~snale~~	snail

If this spelling pattern has any homophones, include these without letting on that both are possible. If one of your students tells you that both are right, tell him or her to write both and then prove it by finding both in the dictionary. When the child has found both, have him or her read the definitions and then help all the students to understand how they can use the dictionary to determine which homophone has the meaning they are trying to spell.

whale	trail
~~jale~~	jail
~~nale~~	nail
scale	~~scail~~
~~snale~~	snail
sale	sail

Continue to add words, interspersing any homophones. At the end of the list, add some longer words to show your students that the same procedure is used for checking the spelling of longer words. If your students are not very quick at finding words in the dictionary, you may want to stop the lesson when they tire and continue it on a second or even a third day.

whale	trail
~~jale~~	jail
~~nale~~	nail
scale	~~scail~~
~~snale~~	snail
sale	sail

stale	~~stail~~
male	mail
bale	bail
~~quale~~	quail
tale	tail
pale	pail
~~fale~~	fail
~~detale~~	detail
~~toenale~~	toenail
exhale	~~exhail~~
~~monorale~~	monorail
~~fingernale~~	fingernail
tattletale	~~tattletail~~

Doing some *What Looks Right?* lessons will take some time but consider all that your students are learning. In addition to developing a visual checking sense, they are learning how to use a dictionary to determine the correct spelling of a word and how the dictionary definitions will tell them which homophone has the meaning they want. You may want to post a chart, "Check Your Spelling," with these strategies after you have done several lessons so that students learn to use these spelling strategies independently when they are writing.

Check Your Spelling

1. If you write a word and it doesn't "look right," try writing the word with a different spelling pattern.

2. If you still are not sure, check the one you think might be right by finding the word in the dictionary.

3. If you are not sure which homophone (sail, sale; deer, dear) to use, find the words in the dictionary and read the definitions to decide which one is right.

In addition to *whale* and *trail*, your word wall contains four other pairs of words you can use as key words for *What Looks Right?* lessons. Here are some lessons for *ote, oat; ite, ight; ue, ew;* and *oon, une.*

vote	**float**
~~gote~~	goat
~~bote~~	boat
note	~~noat~~
~~cote~~	coat
tote	~~toat~~
quote	~~quoat~~
~~throte~~	throat
wrote	~~wroat~~
~~ote~~	oat
~~sailbote~~	sailboat
devote	~~devoat~~
remote	~~remoat~~
~~raincote~~	raincoat
~~lifebote~~	lifeboat

white	**tonight**
bite	~~bight~~
~~brite~~	bright
~~tite~~	tight
kite	~~kight~~
~~fite~~	fight
site	sight
~~flite~~	flight
quite	~~quight~~
write	~~wright~~
~~lite~~	light
~~slite~~	slight
~~midnite~~	midnight
invite	~~invight~~
polite	~~polight~~
~~flashlite~~	flashlight
~~bullfite~~	bullfight
termite	~~termight~~
unite	~~unight~~

true	**new**
~~grue~~	grew
~~drue~~	drew
clue	~~clew~~
~~knue~~	knew
glue	~~glew~~
blue	blew
due	dew
cue	~~cew~~
~~chue~~	chew
~~stue~~	stew
~~fue~~	few
~~thrue~~	threw
~~outgrue~~	outgrew
pursue	~~pursew~~
~~curfue~~	curfew
~~unscrue~~	unscrew
~~renue~~	renew
~~cashue~~	cashew

June	**soon**
~~mune~~	moon
~~spune~~	spoon
tune	~~toon~~
~~gune~~	goon
dune	~~doon~~
prune	~~proon~~
~~nune~~	noon
~~balune~~	balloon
~~cartune~~	cartoon
~~platune~~	platoon
~~typhune~~	typhoon
immune	~~immoon~~
~~racune~~	raccoon
~~afternune~~	afternoon
~~babune~~	baboon
~~cocune~~	cocoon
Neptune	~~Neptoon~~

The Second 25 Words

When all your students can spell the first 25 word wall words, you are ready to begin working with the second set. Included in these 25 words are 7 common words that many students have difficulty spelling:

> during   country   either   caught   finally   probably   unusual

Four more pairs of homophones are included:

> our, hour;   by, buy;   break, brake;   threw, through

These words will be key words for more *What Looks Right?* lessons:

> bread, bed;   wheel, meal;   bait, eight, state

To teach your students to capitalize the names of specific states and countries, include the specific key words as well as the general words:

> United States   America   the name of your state

Add these words gradually to your wall—no more than five each week. You can choose the order, but add the homophone pairs in the same week. You may want to spread out the key words for the capitalizing of specific names across the weeks, but be sure to include the parallel examples (state, your state name) in the same week.

On the day you add words, have your students use these words in oral sentences to make sure they can associate meaning with the words. Have them give several sentences for the homophones to make sure they know which word has which meaning. Get your students out of their seats and lead them to cheer for the five words—three times each word. Have them say the word they are cheering at the beginning and end.

"our o-u-r; o-u-r; o-u-r; our"

"hour h-o-u-r; h-o-u-r; h-o-u-r; hour"

"country c-o-u-n-t-r-y; c-o-u-n-t-r-y; c-o-u-n-t-r-y; country"

"America capital A-m-e-r-i-c-a; capital A-m-e-r-i-c-a;
capital A-m-e-r-i-c-a; America"

"United States capital U-n-i-t-e-d capital S-t-a-t-e-s; capital U-n-i-t-e-d
capital S-t-a-t-e-s; capital U-n-i-t-e-d capital S-t-a-t-e-s; United States"

Next, have them write the words as you model correct letter formation.

our
hour
country
America
United States

Focus on these five new words for two days. Each day, ask students to explain why America and United States begin with capital letters, but the word *country* does not. They should be able to explain that America and United States are specific names. Ask them to name some other countries they would begin with a capital letter (Mexico, Canada, and others.) Then spend three days reviewing word wall words. Each day lead your students to cheer for five words but include some old words and some new words. Have your students write a few sentences using at least two of the word wall words.

My cousin lives in another country.
Our country is the United States.

When all your students can spell these five words quickly and automatically, add five more words. Say some sentences using the new words to make sure your students have these words in their oral vocabulary. Lead your students to cheer the new words—three times each:

"through t-h-r-o-u-g-h; t-h-r-o-u-g-h; t-h-r-o-u-g-h; through"

"threw t-h-r-e-w; t-h-r-e-w; t-h-r-e-w; threw"

"wheel w-h-e-e-l; w-h-e-e-l; w-h-e-e-l; wheel"

"meal m-e-a-l; m-e-a-l; m-e-a-l; meal"

"probably p-r-o-b-a-b-l-y; p-r-o-b-a-b-l-y; p-r-o-b-a-b-l-y; probably"

Model how to write the new words and have the students write them.

through
threw
wheel
meal
probably

Focus on these five new words for two days. Spend three days reviewing the old words. Each day lead your students to cheer for five words but include some of the old words and some new words. Have your students write a few sentences using at least two of the word wall words in each.

McDonald's probably has the best meal deal.
My brother threw the ball through the car window.

Continue to add five words each week following these procedures for each group of words:

- Use new words in sentences to make sure your students have them in their oral vocabulary.
- For two days, focus only on the new words by leading your students to cheer for and write the new words.
- Add the specific names and general names in the same week and have your students explain why the specific names are capitalized and give other examples of specific states and countries.
- Add the homophones in the same week and have your students create several oral sentences to show which word has which meaning.
- For three days, choose five words to cheer for, including some old words and some new words.
- Have your students write a few sentences that include at least two of the word wall words.

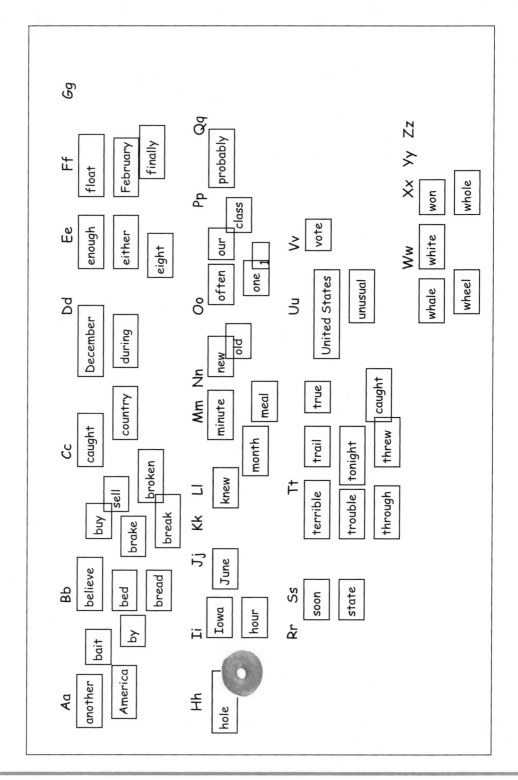

Review the First 50 Words

When you have 50 words on your wall, take a few weeks to review your word wall words and teach rhyming patterns and spelling changes. Have students choose 25 of the 50 word wall words to write on their WORDO sheet. Call out words from the wall until someone has covered all the words on his or her card. Be sure to give clues to the homophones so the students know which one to cover. Check to see that all the words they covered were called and they are all spelled correctly on their sheet. If you have time, have the students clear their card and play another round.

whole	probably	believe	trouble	brake
through	wheel	tonight	unusual	threw
bed	February	finally	enough	float
bread	often	eight	break	America
another	minute	month	Iowa	trail

Teaching Your Students to Capitalize Specific Nouns

Remind students that specific names, including the names of people, places, holidays, months, and days of the week begin with capital letters. Write the words *America* and *United States* under the word *country* and the state you have added to your word wall under the word *state*. Have students brainstorm other states and countries and write these under the appropriate word to help them see that all the names of specific countries and states begin with capital letters.

This is the last time in these lessons that capitalizing specific nouns is taught. You may want to extend your students' understanding about capitalizing specific nouns by including some other general noun categories and having your students name specific local examples and showing them how the specific examples always begin with capital letters. They could work in pairs or trios to add more examples to a chart such as the following:

state	country	continent	park	store	restaurant
North Carolina	Mexico	Asia	Rock Creek Park	Food Lion	Red Lobster

● Teaching the Homophones

Add the sets of homophones in the same week. Put a clue on one of them so your students will learn which word has which meaning. For *our* and *hour*, attach a card with the clue *our class* next to *our*. For *threw* and *through*, attach a card next to *threw* with the word *caught* on it and explain, "This is the *threw* that is the opposite of *caught*." For *by* and *buy*, attach a card next to *buy* with the word *sell* on it and explain, "This is the *buy* that is the opposite of *sell*." For *break* and *brake*, attach a card with the clue *broken* on it and explain that when you *break* something, it is broken.

● What Looks Right? Lessons

In addition to lessons with the words taught in this set, *state, eight, bait; wheel, meal; bread,* you can teach a *What Looks Right?* lesson using two previously taught words, *street* and *eat.* Write these words on your chart or board and have your students write the same words in columns on their papers.

street   eat

Have your students pronounce and spell the words and remind them some rhymes have two common spelling patterns. Highlight or underline the spelling pattern in *street* and *eat* and have them do the same on their papers. Next, say a word that rhymes with *street* and *eat* and write it both ways, saying, "If the word is spelled like *street,* it will be c-h-e-e-t. If it is spelled like *eat,* it will be c-h-e-a-t." Write these two possible spellings under the appropriate word.

street   eat
cheet   cheat

Tell your students to decide which one "looks right" to them and to write **only the one** they think is correct. When the students have decided which one looks right and have written this word in the correct column, ask your students to find the word in the dictionary to "prove they are right." Don't wait for everyone to find the correct spelling. As soon as anyone has found it, ask all your students to turn to that page and verify the correct spelling. If any of your students guessed wrong, have them erase the incorrect spelling and write the correct spelling. Cross out the spelling you wrote that is not correct and continue with another example.

For the first examples, choose common words that you think most of your students will instantly recognize which is the correct spelling. As you write each word, explain your thinking. "If it is spelled like *street*, it will be s-w-e-e-t, but if it is spelled like *eat*, it will be s-w-e-a-t."

street	eat
~~cheet~~	cheat
sweet	sweat

After you have written the word both ways, have your students choose the one they think is correct and write only that one. When they have made their choice, tell them to find the word in the dictionary to prove they were correct and then fix any incorrect spellings. Cross out your incorrect spelling.

street	eat
~~cheet~~	cheat
sweet	~~sweat~~

Continue to add words and have your students guess and then check. As the lesson goes on, they should get quicker at finding the words in the dictionary.

street	eat
~~cheet~~	cheat
sweet	~~sweat~~
sheet	~~sheat~~
~~neet~~	neat

If this spelling pattern has any homophones, include them without letting on that both are possible. If some students tell you that both are right, tell them they can write both and then prove it by finding both in the dictionary. When the children have found both, have them read the definitions and then help them understand how they can use the dictionary to determine which homophone has the meaning they are trying to spell.

street	eat
~~cheet~~	cheat
sweet	~~sweat~~
sheet	~~sheat~~
~~neet~~	neat
meet	meat

Continue to add words, interspersing any homophones. At the end of the list, add some longer words to show your students that the same procedure is used for checking the spelling of longer words. If your students are not very quick at finding words in the dictionary, you may want to stop the lesson when they tire and continue it on a second or even a third day.

street	eat
~~cheet~~	cheat
sweet	~~sweat~~
sheet	~~sheat~~
~~neet~~	neat
meet	meat
greet	~~great~~
sleet	~~sleat~~
~~wheet~~	wheat
beet	beat
~~seet~~	seat
feet	feat
tweet	~~tweat~~
fleet	~~fleat~~
~~retreet~~	retreat
~~heartbeet~~	heartbeat
~~backseet~~	backseat
~~mistreet~~	mistreat
~~repeet~~	repeat
parakeet	~~parakeat~~

Here are some lessons for *eal, eel; ed, ead;* and *ait, ate, eight.*

meal	wheel	bed	bread
~~feal~~	feel	~~hed~~	head
seal	~~seel~~	~~ded~~	dead
~~kneal~~	kneel	red	read
heal	heel	shed	~~shead~~
teal	~~teel~~	~~spred~~	spread
steal	steel	sled	~~slead~~
squeal	~~squeel~~	led	lead
peal	peel	fled	~~flead~~
~~eal~~	eel	~~dred~~	dread
real	reel	shred	~~shread~~
appeal	~~appeel~~	~~thred~~	thread
oatmeal	~~oatmeel~~	fed	~~fead~~
~~cartwheal~~	cartwheel	~~ahed~~	ahead
ideal	~~ideel~~	~~gingerbred~~	gingerbread
		~~insted~~	instead
		bunkbed	~~bunkbead~~
		thoroughbred	~~thoroughbread~~
		moped	~~mopead~~
		redhed	redhead

bait	state	eight
~~dait~~	date	~~deight~~
~~hait~~	hate	~~height~~
wait	~~wate~~	weight
~~stait~~	state	~~steight~~
~~mait~~	mate	~~meight~~
~~skait~~	skate	~~skeight~~
~~frait~~	~~frate~~	freight
~~plait~~	plate	~~pleight~~
~~crait~~	crate	~~creight~~
gait	gate	~~geight~~
~~lait~~	late	~~leight~~
~~rait~~	rate	~~reight~~
~~evacuait~~	evacuate	~~evacueight~~
~~overwait~~	~~overwate~~	overweight
~~hibernait~~	hibernate	~~hiberneight~~
~~inflait~~	inflate	~~infleight~~
~~lightwait~~	~~lightwate~~	lightweight
~~amputait~~	amputate	~~amputeight~~
~~rebait~~	rebate	~~rebeight~~

How Can I Look It Up in the Dictionary if I Can't Spell It?

Do your students ever look at you strangely when you tell them to look up a word they don't know how to spell? They are probably wondering how they can look up a word if they can't spell it. In reality, you can almost always come up with the first several letters of a word you are unsure about and often you can come up with a probable spelling. In addition to helping your students develop a visual checking sense, *What Looks Right?* lessons teach your students how to use dictionaries to determine the correct spelling of a word.

The Third 25 Words

When all your students can spell the first 50 key words, you are ready to begin working with the third set. The third set of 25 words contains 5 common words that many students have difficulty spelling:

    picture   million   thousand   vacation   answer

Three more pairs of homophones are included:

    piece peace   close clothes   sun son

Five key words allow you to review spelling changes and teach *er* (person), *er, est,* and *en* endings:

    winner   biggest   happier   hidden   exciting

Nine words will be key words for more *What Looks Right?* lessons:

    afraid   grade   train   crane   year   cheer   green   mean   machine

Add these words gradually to your wall—no more than five each week. Add the homophone pairs in the same week. When you add words with endings and spelling changes, talk about the meaning the ending adds to the words and spelling changes.

On the day you add words, have your students use these words in oral sentences to make sure they can associate meaning with the words. Have them give several sentences for the homophones to make sure they know which word has which meaning. Get your students out of their seats and lead them to cheer for the five words—three times each word. Have them say the word they are cheering at the beginning and end.

    "vacation v-a-c-a-t-i-o-n; v-a-c-a-t-i-o-n; v-a-c-a-t-i-o-n; vacation"

    "peace p-e-a-c-e; p-e-a-c-e; p-e-a-c-e; peace"

    "piece p-i-e-c-e; p-i-e-c-e; p-i-e-c-e; piece"

    "biggest b-i-g-g-e-s-t; b-i-g-g-e-s-t; b-i-g-g-e-s-t; biggest"

    "happier h-a-p-p-i-e-r; h-a-p-p-i-e-r; h-a-p-p-i-e-r; happier"

Next, have them write the words as you model correct letter formation.

vacation

peace

piece

biggest

happier

Focus on these five new words for two days. Each day, ask students what *er* and *est* mean when added to words. Have them give examples of other words to which they can add *er* and *est* and add the meaning of more or most (sad, funny, deep, etc.). Ask them to tell you how they would spell their example words when adding *er* and *est* and if any spelling changes are required. Then spend three days reviewing the old words. Each day lead your students to cheer for five words but include some old words and some new words. Have your students write a few sentences using at least two of the word wall words.

I got the biggest piece of cake because it was my birthday.

On our vacation, my family drove through eight states.

When all your students can spell these five words quickly and automatically, add five more words. Have your students use these words in oral sentences to make sure they can associate meaning with the words. Tell them to give several sentences for the homophones to make sure they know which word has which meaning. Lead your students to cheer the new words—three times each:

"close c-l-o-s-e; c-l-o-s-e; c-l-o-s-e; close"

"clothes c-l-o-t-h-e-s; c-l-o-t-h-e-s; c-l-o-t-h-e-s; clothes"

"answer a-n-s-w-e-r; a-n-s-w-e-r; a-n-s-w-e-r; answer"

"afraid a-f-r-a-i-d; a-f-r-a-i-d; a-f-r-a-i-d; afraid"

"grade g-r-a-d-e; g-r-a-d-e; g-r-a-d-e; grade"

Model how to write the new words and have the students write them.

close

clothes

answer

afraid

grade

Focus on these five new words for two days. Then spend three days reviewing the old words. Each day lead your students to cheer for five words but include some old words and some new words. Have your students write a few sentences using at least two of the word wall words.

I knew the right answer.

When we go on vacation, my mom is afraid people might break into our house.

Spelling Skills Help Only if the Students Use Them When They Write!

The only reason your children need to learn how to spell words is to enable them to write fluently and well. If they learn to spell words during your spelling practice but do not spell them correctly when writing, your spelling practice is wasted. Provide weekly practice spelling the word wall words as they write a few sentences. When they are writing throughout the day, remind them to use the word wall and hold them accountable for spelling word wall words correctly in everything they write.

Continue to add five words each week following these procedures for each group of words.

- Use new words in sentences to make sure your students have them in their oral vocabulary.
- For two days, focus only on the new words by leading your students to cheer for and write the new words.
- Add the homophones in the same week and have your students create several oral sentences to show which word has which meaning.
- For three days, choose five words to cheer for, including some old words and some new words.
- Have your students write sentences that include at least two of the word wall words.

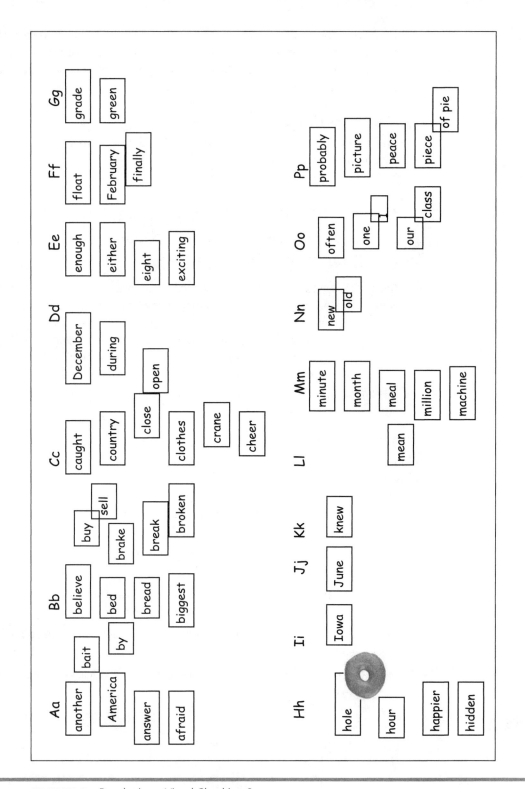

Aa
another
bait
America
by
answer
afraid

Bb
believe
bed
buy
sell
bread
brake
biggest
break
broken

Cc
caught
country
close
open
clothes
crane
cheer

Dd
December
during

Ee
enough
either
eight
exciting

Ff
float
February
finally

Gg
grade
green

Hh
hole
hour
happier
hidden

Ii
Iowa

Jj
June

Kk
knew

Ll
minute
month
mean
meal
million
machine

Mm
(see Ll list)

Nn
new
old

Oo
often
one
our
class

Pp
probably
picture
peace
piece
of pie

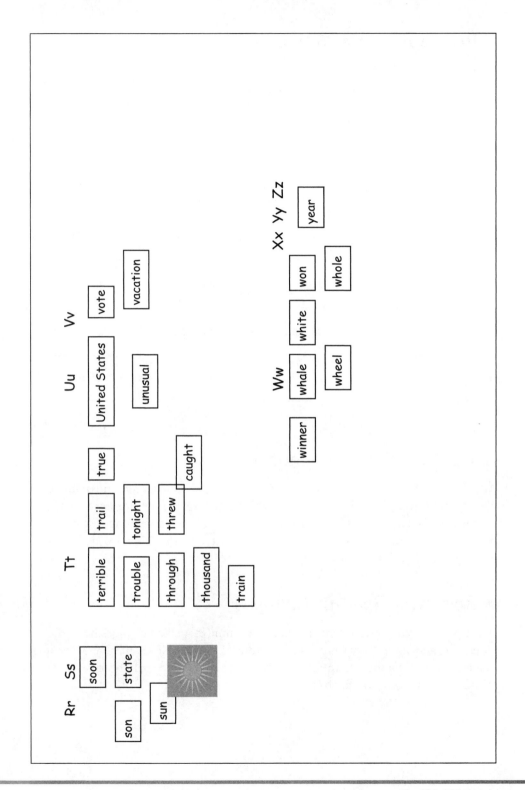

Rr

Ss
- son
- soon
- state
- sun

Tt
- terrible
- trail
- true
- trouble
- tonight
- through
- threw
- caught
- thousand
- train

Uu
- United States
- unusual

Vv
- vote
- vacation

Ww
- winner
- whale
- white
- won
- wheel
- whole

Xx Yy Zz
- year

● Review the First 75 Words

When you have 75 words on your wall, take a few weeks to review your word wall words. Have students create WORDO sheets by choosing 25 of the 75 word wall words. Call words until someone has all his or her words covered. Check to see that the words were called and they are all spelled correctly.

piece	cheer	believe	trouble	brake
peace	machine	exciting	picture	meal
biggest	February	finally	million	crane
happier	often	afraid	hidden	America
restaurant	together	vacation	special	winner

● Teaching the Homophones

Add the sets of homophones in the same week. Put a clue on all but one of them so your students will learn which word has which meaning. For *son* and *sun,* attach a card with the picture of a sun next to *sun.* For *piece* and *piece,* attach the clue *piece of pie* next to *piece.* For *close* and *close,* attach a card next to *close* with the word *open* on it and explain, "This is the *close* that is the opposite of *open.*"

● Reviewing Spelling Changes

In the previous chapter, students learned the common spelling changes needed when *s, ed,* and *ing* endings were added to words. Extend their knowledge of spelling changes by drawing their attention to the spelling changes to spell these key words. Write each key word with the base word next to it.

winner	win
hidden	hid
biggest	big
happiest	happy
exciting	excite

Remind students of spelling changes they have learned and ask them which ones apply to which key words.

- Double the letter if it follows a single vowel or consonant.
- Change the *y* to *i* when adding an ending that begins with a vowel.
- Drop the *e* when adding an ending that begins with a vowel.

Write these words on index cards and have students write them on a WORDO sheet.

sharp	noisy	late	dark	tiny
cute	nice	mad	run	safe
sad	sleepy	WORDO	flip	bat
camp	catch	hot	surprise	pitch
sharp	sad	mean	clean	quit

Show each index card and say the word with the endings shown on the next WORDO sheet. Ask the students to tell you how to spell the word with the ending. Write that ending on the index card and have the students add the endings on their WORDO sheets, including spelling changes as needed. Shuffle the deck of index cards and call out the words. Be sure that anyone who wins has the words spelled correctly—including spelling changes—on the WORDO sheet.

sharpen	noisier	later	darkest	tiniest
cutest	nicest	madder	runner	safest
sadden	sleepiest	WORDO	flipper	batter
camper	catcher	hotter	surprising	pitcher
sharpest	saddest	meanest	cleaner	quitter

● What Looks Right? Lessons

The words in this set will allow you to teach four more *What Looks Right?* lessons with words that have two or three common spelling patterns. Here are words you might use for those lessons.

afraid	grade	train	crane
traid	trade	cain	cane
paid	pade	lain	lane
raid	rade	brain	brane
waid	wade	sain	sane
maid	made	pain	pane
braid	brade	rain	rane
aid	ade	plain	plane
spaid	spade	chain	chane
shaid	shade	strain	strane
faid	fade	sprain	sprane
blaid	blade	main	mane
mermaid	mermade	grain	grane
bridesmaid	bridesmade	explain	explane
arcaid	arcade	complain	complane
paraid	parade	airplain	airplane
barricaid	barricade	remain	remain
blockaid	blockade	insain	insane
lemonaid	lemonade	contain	contane
lampshaid	lampshade		

year	cheer
ear	~~eer~~
~~stear~~	steer
near	~~neer~~
dear	deer
gear	~~geer~~
year	~~yeer~~
spear	~~speer~~
hear	~~heer~~
clear	~~cleer~~
~~reindear~~	reindeer
appear	~~appeer~~
~~pinoear~~	pioneer
~~enginear~~	engineer
~~voluntear~~	volunteer
disappear	~~disappeer~~

green	mean	machine
~~cleen~~	clean	~~cline~~
teen	~~tean~~	~~tine~~
~~been~~	bean	~~bine~~
queen	~~quean~~	~~quine~~
~~leen~~	lean	~~line~~
screen	~~screan~~	~~scrine~~
seen	~~sean~~	~~sine~~
~~deen~~	dean	~~dine~~
keen	~~kean~~	~~kine~~
between	~~betwean~~	~~betwine~~
~~sardeen~~	~~sardean~~	sardine
~~submareen~~	~~submarean~~	submarine
fifteen	~~fiftean~~	~~fiftine~~
sunscreen	~~sunscrean~~	~~sunscrine~~
~~magazeen~~	~~magazean~~	magazine
~~routeen~~	~~routean~~	routine
nineteen	~~ninetean~~	~~ninetine~~
~~jellybeen~~	jellybean	~~jellybine~~
~~trampoleen~~	~~trampolean~~	trampoline
~~tamboureen~~	~~tambourean~~	tambourine
seventeen	~~seventean~~	~~seventine~~

The Final 25 Words

When all your students can spell the first 75 word wall words, you are ready to begin working with the final set. The final set contains 8 common words that many students have difficulty spelling:

neighbor   restaurant   thought   together   special   interesting   listen   although

Four compound words are key words for many other compound words:

however   anyone   something   everybody

Three more pairs of common homophones are included:

accept   except   weather   whether   bear   bare

Seven words are key words for *What Looks Right?* lessons:

chair   phone   own   loan   code   unload   snowed

Add these words gradually to your wall—no more than five each week. Add the homophone pairs in the same week.

On the day you add words, have your students use these words in oral sentences to make sure they can associate meaning with the words. Have them give several sentences for the homophones to make sure they know which word has which meaning. Get your students out of their seats and lead them to cheer for the five words—three times each word. Have them say the word they are cheering at the beginning and end.

"neighbor n-e-i-g-h-b-o-r; n-e-i-g-h-b-o-r; n-e-i-g-h-b-o-r; neighbor"

"thought t-h-o-u-g-h-t; t-h-o-u-g-h-t; t-h-o-u-g-h-t; thought"

"however h-o-w-e-v-e-r; h-o-w-e-v-e-r; h-o-w-e-v-e-r; however "

"accept a-c-c-e-p-t; a-c-c-e-p-t; a-c-c-e-p-t; accept"

"except e-x-c-e-p-t; e-x-c-e-p-t; e-x-c-e-p-t; except"

Next, have them write the words as you model correct letter formation.

neighbor

thought

however

accept

except

Focus on these five new words for two days. Then spend three days reviewing the old words. Each day lead your students to cheer for five words but include some old words and some new words. Have your students write a few sentences using at least two of the word wall words.

Our neighbors moved to the United States from another country.

All the children were afraid except me.

When all your students can spell these five words quickly and automatically, add five more words. Have your students use these words in oral sentences to make sure they can associate meaning with the words. Lead your students to cheer the new words—three times each:

"restaurant r-e-s-t-a-u-r-a-n-t; r-e-s-t-a-u-r-a-n-t; r-e-s-t-a-u-r-a-n-t; restaurant"

"special s-p-e-c-i-a-l; s-p-e-c-i-a-l; s-p-e-c-i-a-l; special"

"everybody e-v-e-r-y-b-o-d-y; e-v-e-r-y-b-o-d-y; e-v-e-r-y-b-o-d-y; everybody"

"something s-o-m-e-t-h-i-n-g; s-o-m-e-t-h-i-n-g; s-o-m-e-t-h-i-n-g; something"

"anyone a-n-y-o-n-e; a-n-y-o-n-e; a-n-y-o-n-e; anyone"

Model how to write the new words and have the students write them.

restaurant

special

everybody

something

anyone

Focus on these five new words for two days. Then spend three days reviewing the old words. Each day lead your students to cheer for five words but include some old words and some new words. Have your students write a few sentences using at least two of the word wall words.

Everybody thought the new restaurant was great.
In art, we drew a picture of something special.

Continue to add five words each week following these procedures for each group of words.

- Use new words in sentences to make sure your students have them in their oral vocabulary.
- For two days, focus only on the new words by leading your students to cheer for and write the new words.
- Add the homophones in the same week and have your students create several oral sentences to show which word has which meaning.
- For three days, choose five words to cheer for, including some old words and some new words.
- Have your students write a few sentences that include at least two of the word wall words.

● Teaching the Homophones

Add the sets of homophones in the same week. Put a clue on one of them so your students will learn which word has which meaning. For *accept* and *except,* attach a card next to *accept* with a sentence such as, *I accept!* For *whether* and *weather,* attach a card next to *weather* with a picture of sun and clouds. For *bear* and *bare,* attach a card next to *bear* with a picture of a bear.

● What Looks Right? Lessons

The words in this set will allow you to teach three more *What Looks Right?* lessons with words that have two or three common spelling patterns. Here are words you might use for those lessons.

chair	bare
~~squair~~	square
air	~~are~~
pair	pare
~~cair~~	care
fair	fare
stair	stare
~~dair~~	dare
~~mair~~	mare
~~scair~~	scare
~~shair~~	share
hair	hare
~~rair~~	rare
affair	~~affare~~
~~prepair~~	prepare
~~nightmair~~	nightmare
~~compair~~	compare
~~awair~~	aware
repair	~~repare~~
wheelchair	~~wheelchare~~
unfair	~~unfare~~

phone	own	loan
~~knone~~	known	~~knoan~~
bone	~~bown~~	~~boan~~
cone	~~cown~~	~~coan~~
~~grone~~	grown	groan
clone	~~clown~~	~~cloan~~
zone	~~zown~~	~~zoan~~
~~flone~~	flown	~~floan~~
tone	~~town~~	~~toan~~
drone	~~drown~~	~~droan~~
stone	~~stown~~	~~stoan~~
~~mone~~	~~mown~~	moan
throne	thrown	~~throan~~
alone	~~alown~~	~~aloan~~
postpone	~~postpown~~	~~postpoan~~
microphone	~~microphown~~	~~microphoan~~
backbone	~~backbown~~	~~backboan~~
headphone	~~headphown~~	~~headphoan~~
trombone	~~trombown~~	~~tromboan~~
cyclone	~~cyclown~~	~~cycloan~~
~~windblone~~	windblown	~~windbloan~~
hormone	~~hormown~~	~~hormoan~~

code	unload	snowed
mode	~~moad~~	mowed
rode	road	rowed
~~tode~~	toad	towed
~~shode~~	~~shoad~~	showed
~~glode~~	~~gload~~	glowed
~~flode~~	~~fload~~	flowed
~~crode~~	~~croad~~	crowed
~~stode~~	~~stoad~~	stowed
erode	~~eroad~~	~~erowed~~
explode	~~expload~~	~~explowed~~
episode	~~episoad~~	~~episowed~~
~~overflode~~	~~overfload~~	overflowed
~~trucklode~~	truckload	~~trucklowed~~
~~railrode~~	railroad	~~railrowed~~
~~unlode~~	unload	~~unlowed~~
~~crossrode~~	crossroad	~~crossrowed~~

Review, Consolidate, Celebrate!

When your students can spell the 100 key words in this chapter, they should be able to spell many illogically spelled common words and be automatic at capitalizing the first letter of specific nouns. They should have developed a visual checking sense, learned the meaning and spelling for common homophones, and learned how to use the dictionary to check the spelling of a word and determine homophone meanings. Take as much time as you can in the final weeks of school to review the words, help them consolidate their spelling strategies, and celebrate their spelling prowess!

● WORDO for Key Words

You can use the WORDO game format to review the word wall words. Have students choose 24 of the 100 key words and write them in the squares. Shuffle a deck of 100 index cards with key words written on them and call out words until someone wins. Check to be sure that all covered words that have been called and that the words are spelled correctly. You can play for rows, columns, diagonals, or a full card.

special	thousand	whale	trail	weather
February	interesting	mean	million	trouble
clothes	caught	**WORDO**	tonight	neighbor
December	everybody	hidden	machine	peace
through	during	exciting	unload	phone

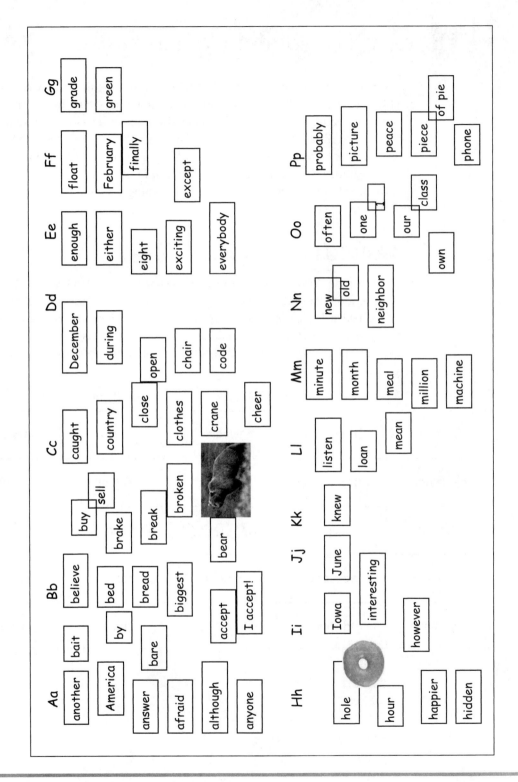

Aa
another, bait, America, by, bare, answer, afraid, although, anyone

Bb
believe, bed, bread, biggest, accept, I accept!, buy, sell, brake, break, broken, bear

Cc
caught, country, close, open, clothes, chair, crane, code, cheer

Dd
December, during

Ee
enough, either, eight, exciting, everybody

Ff
float, February, finally, except

Gg
grade, green

Hh
hole, hour, happier, hidden, however

Ii
Iowa, interesting

Jj
June

Kk
knew

Ll
listen, loan, mean

Mm
minute, month, meal, million, machine

Nn
new, old, neighbor

Oo
often, one, our, class, own

Pp
probably, picture, peace, piece, of pie, phone

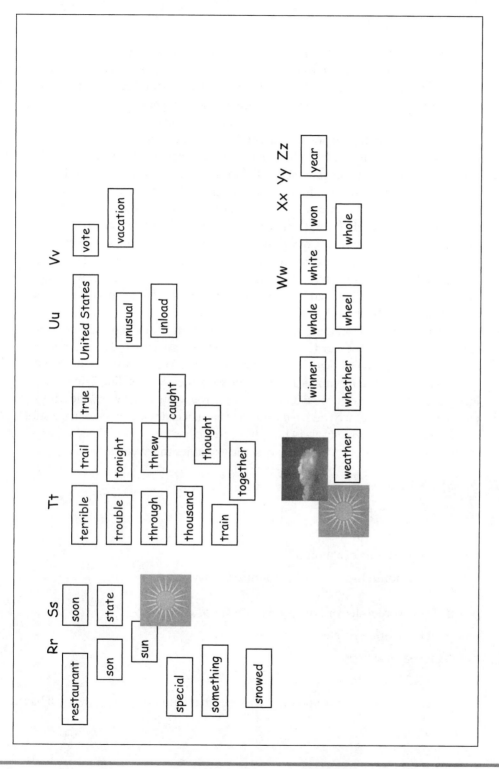

Rr

- restaurant

Ss

- son
- soon
- sun
- state
- special
- something
- snowed

Tt

- terrible
- trail
- true
- trouble
- tonight
- through
- threw
- caught
- thousand
- thought
- train
- together
- weather

Uu

- United States
- unusual
- unload

Vv

- vote
- vacation

Ww

- winner
- whale
- white
- won
- whether
- wheel
- whole

Xx Yy Zz

- year

● Be a Mind Reader

Be a Mind Reader is another game you can use to review word wall words. In this game, you think of a word on the wall and then give five clues to that word. Choose a word and write it on a scrap of paper but do not let the students see what word you have written. Tell each student to number a piece of paper from 1 to 5. Explain that you are going to see who can read your mind and figure out which of the words on the wall you are thinking of and have written on your paper. Tell them you will give them five clues. By the fifth clue, everyone should guess your word, but if they read your mind they might get it before the fifth clue. Since you now have 100 words on your wall and your students' names, give a first clue which limits the words to 6 or 7 alphabet letters. Tell your students to write next to number 1 the word they think it might be. Each succeeding clue should narrow down what it can be until by clue 5 there is only one possible word. As you give clues, students write the word they believe it is next to each number. If succeeding clues confirm the word a student has written next to one number, the student writes that word again by the next number. If succeeding clues eliminate the word, students choose a new word that fits all the clues.

After clue 5, show students the word you wrote on your scrap paper and say, "I know you all have the word next to number 5 but who has it next to number 4? 3? 2? 1?" All students who guessed the word on line 1 are the winners. If no one guessed it on line 1, the winners are everyone who guessed it on line 2. In the unlikely event that no one guessed it on line 1 or 2, the winners are everyone who guessed it on line 3. Once you have your winners, check their papers to make sure the word is spelled correctly every time. If someone has not spelled the word correctly, he or she does not win! Here are some examples to get you started.

1. It's a word wall word that starts with *a, b, c, d, e,* or *f.*
2. It has 7 or more letters.
3. It does not begin with *c.*
4. It is the name of a month.
5. This month has the smallest number of days.

1. It's a word wall word that starts with *t, u, v, w, x, y,* or *z.*
2. It has 6 or more letters.
3. It begins with *w.*
4. It is a homophone.
5. Every morning I turn on the TV to see what kind of _____ we will have.

1. It's a word wall word that starts with *g, h, i, j, k, l,* or *m.*
2. It does not have an *h.*
3. It has 5 or fewer letters.
4. It begins with *g.*
5. It is my favorite color.

1. It's a word wall word that starts with *n, o, p, q, r, s,* or *t.*
2. It has 7 letters.
3. It does not begin with *p.*
4. It does not begin with *s.*
5. This is something you do NOT want to be in!

● Spelling by Pattern and Visual Checking Sense

By now your students should be using rhyming patterns from all the words they know to spell new words. When there are two common spellings for one rhyme, they should write the word the way they think it is spelled and then look to see if it "looks right." If, however, they have never seen the word before—or seen it very few times—they won't know if it looks right. That is when dictionaries are most useful. We don't look up a word in the dictionary because we have no idea how to spell it. We look it up to see which possible spelling is the correct one.

Key words for the most common rhymes with two or three common spellings were taught in this chapter and your students should have learned how to use their visual checking sense and a dictionary to determine correct spellings. This chart lists the key words with two or three common spelling patterns and other words your students should be able to spell.

Note: Rhyming patterns are highlighted.

Key words	Words they should be able to spell using patterns and visual checking sense
whale	bale male pale sale scale stale exhale inhale
trail	bail fail jail mail nail quail pail sail snail tail detail
vote	note quote wrote remote
float	boat coat goat oat throat sailboat raincoat

tonight	bright tight fight sight flight light slight midnight
white	bite kite site quite invite unite polite
soon	moon goon noon spoon cartoon balloon baboon afternoon
June	tune dune prune
true	blue clue cue due glue
new	grew drew knew blew dew chew stew few threw outgrew renew
eat	cheat neat meat wheat beat seat feat retreat repeat
street	sweet sheet meet greet sleet beet feet tweet fleet
state	date hate mate skate plate crate gate late rate inflate rebate
bait	wait gait
eight	weight freight overweight lightweight
bread	read dead head spread tread dread lead ahead instead redhead
bed	red shed sled led fled fed moped bunkbed
wheel	feel heel steel eel kneel reel cartwheel
meal	seal teal heal steal squeal oatmeal ideal
afraid	paid braid maid aid raid
grade	trade wade made spade shade fade blade parade blockade
train	brain pain rain plain chain strain sprain main grain explain remain
crane	cane lane sane pane plane mane insane airplane
year	ear near dear gear year spear hear clear
cheer	deer steer
green	teen queen screen keen seen between fifteen nineteen
mean	clean bean lean dean
bare	square care fare stare dare mare scare share hare rare prepare nightmare

chair	air pair fair stair hair repair unfair
phone	bone cone clone zone tone drone stone throne alone backbone headphone
loan	groan moan
own	grown known flown thrown
snowed	glowed showed stowed crowed rowed mowed towed flowed overflowed
code	code mode rode erode explode
unload	load toad road truckload unload

Choose from the words on this chart to create a WORDO game and review visual checking sense. Call out 24 of the new words and ask students to use a rhyming word wall word to spell the words and write them on their WORDO sheets. After they write each word, ask them if it looks right to them and which alternate pattern they might have used. If there is any disagreement among your students about which spelling is correct, have them find the word in the dictionary to prove they are correct. When calling out a homophone such as *fare* or *fair,* provide a sentence clue so the students know which word they are trying to spell. Again, if there is any disagreement, have them use the dictionary to determine which homophone has which meaning. Write the words you call out on index cards. When you have called out and confirmed the spelling of 24 words, shuffle the deck and play a few rounds of WORDO.

fleet	airplane	repair	parade	remain
spread	cartwheel	inflate	balloon	unload
squeal	throne	WORDO	sled	stare
overweight	nineteen	steel	shade	invite
tweet	stew	code	deer	nightmare

● Other Words Your Students Can Spell Based on Key Words

The chart below lists other words your students should be able to spell based on your word wall words. Call out 24 new words and have students decide which word wall word will help them spell them. Write the words you call out on index cards and have students choose a place on their WORDO sheets to write them.

Key words	Other words they should be able to spell
another	other brother mother grandmother stepmother stepbrother smother
enough	rough tough
trouble	double
tonight	today
either	neither
finally	final
probably	probable
unusual	usual usually unusually
picture	nature future capture mixture pasture texture torture vulture
million	billion trillion zillion
vacation	notion lotion nation action option potion ration caption emotion mention portion station fiction section suction
winner	scanner planner spinner runner gunner beginner
biggest	saddest maddest thinnest fattest fittest flattest hottest wettest
happier	prettier muddier sloppier
exciting	excited
neighbor	neighborly neighborhood
thought	ought bought brought fought

however	ever never sever lever clever forever whoever whatever whenever wherever
anyone	anybody anything anywhere anyhow anytime
something	somebody somewhere somehow sometimes somehow somewhat
everybody	everyone everything everywhere
weather	feather leather

leather	somebody	anyhow	stepbrother	tough
planner	saddest	trillion	probable	usual
muddier	neighborly	WORDO	whatever	nation
spinner	anytime	everything	thinnest	section
usual	today	clever	sloppier	somehow

● Make a Homophone Book

Here is a chance for your artistic children to shine. Have your students choose a set of homophones and write a sentence for each homophone or one sentence that contains both homophones. Have them illustrate their sentences and put them together in a class book. Ask your students to select from the homophones included in the word wall or taught in *What Looks Right?* lessons. Your advanced students might want to look up some new homophones in the dictionary and create pages for them.

Homophones taught in this chapter and previous chapter		
accept except	ate eight	bale bail
bear bare	beet beat	blue blew
break brake	by buy	close clothes
dear deer	do due dew	fair fare
feet feat	gait gate	groan grown
hair hare	heal heel	hear here
hole whole	led lead	maid made
main mane	male mail	meet meat
new knew	no know	once wants
one won	our hour	pain pane
pale pail	peal peel	piece peace
plain plane	real reel	red read
right write	road rode rowed	sale sail
site sight	stare stair	steal steel
sun son	tale tail	there their they're
threw through	throne thrown	to too two
toad towed	wait weight	wear where we're
weather whether		

Other common homophones			
ad add	ant aunt	ball bawl	band banned
be bee	berry bury	board bored	bolder boulder
choose chews	flee flea	flew flu	flour flower
for four	great grate	hall haul	heard herd
hi high	horse hoarse	in inn	need knead
night knight	pair pear	rain rein reign	rap wrap
roll role	rose rows	sea see	sell cell
sent cent scent	sore soar	steak stake	tied tide
war wore	we wee	which witch	wood would

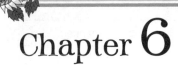

Chapter 6

Building Meaning, Phonics, and Spelling Skills for Big Words

"Why does *bomb* have a *b* at the end and *sign* have a *g*?"

"Why is there a *c* in *muscle*?"

"Why is the second syllable of *composition* spelled with an *o* but a syllable that sounds the same in *competition* is spelled with an *e*?"

The answer to these questions is that spelling preserves the meaning linkages across words. The *b* at the end of *bomb* maintains the meaning relationship between bomb and other "relatives" such as *bombard* and *bombastic*. *Signal*, *signature*, and other related words will explain the *g* in *sign*, and *muscular* will explain the *c* in *muscle*. The middle syllable of *composition* is spelled with an *o* because of its relationship to *compose*. Likewise, *competition* is related to *compete*. Linguists believe that English spelling is more dependent on morphology than any other language. Most English morphemes have a single spelling even though their pronunciations vary. The past tense of *walked, crawled,* and *dated* all end with the *e-d* pattern, but those endings have three different pronunciations. Vowels change pronunciations as word form changes, shown by the pronunciation of the *a* in *volcano* when it becomes *volcanic*. In many other languages, the spelling would reflect these changes in pronunciation. But in English, spelling maintains meaning links at the expense of sound (O'Grady, Dobrovolsky, & Aronoff, 1989). Templeton (1991) put it most succinctly when he said students need to learn that "words that are related in meaning are often related in spelling as well, despite changes in sound" (p. 194). In fact, when it comes to spelling big words, meaning, not sound, rules! In order to become a good speller from fourth grade on, you must abandon a "memorize the letters" strategy or a "write down the letters that stand for the sound" strategy and realize that even those patterns that work in short words often don't work in longer words. You need to develop a strategy in which you consider at some level what words might be related to this word.

The First 25 Big Words and Their Parts

Big words are a challenge for even the best of spellers. When writing, they often use the short words they can spell rather than longer words that would be more descriptive but that they might not be able to spell. They describe animals as very "big" rather than "enormous" or "gigantic" not because they don't know the words *enormous* or *gigantic* but because they are unsure how to spell them. Many long words are just shorter words with chunks—often prefixes and suffixes—added at the beginning and end. *International*—a very long and scary word for most elementary students—is easy to spell if you recognize that it is made up of the prefix *inter,* the root word *nation,* and the suffix *al*. To spell *replacement*, you begin with the prefix *re,* and then add the root word *place* and the suffix *ment*. Some big words end with unusual spellings. Many older students would spell *explosion* and *attention exploshun* and *attenshun*. Some longer words do not have recognizable prefixes and suffixes but they do have predictable chunks.

The patterns in long words are often different from the patterns in short words. Short words such as *lick, brick, sick, trick,* and others are spelled with the *i-c-k* patterns. This same sound and syllable, when found at the end of long words, is spelled *i-c*. Almost all long words that end like *gigantic* end in *ic—electric, organic, athletic, magnetic,* and so on. Short words such as *us, bus, fuss,* and *muss* are spelled with the *u-s* or *u-s-s* pattern. In longer words, however, that same sound is commonly spelled *o-u-s*. Almost all long words that sound like the last syllable in *enormous* end with *ous: nervous, dangerous, fabulous, ridiculous,* and so on.

If we are to teach the word parts that are most useful, we must know what these are. White, Sowell, and Yanagihara (1989) analyzed the words from the Carroll, Davies, and Richman (1971) word frequency study and found that 20 prefixes accounted for 97 percent of the prefixed words. Four prefixes—*un, re, in* (and *im, ir, il* meaning "not") and *dis*—accounted for 58 percent of all prefixed words. The prefixes accounting for the other 39 percent of the words were *en/em, non, in/im* (meaning "in"), *over, mis, sub, pre, inter, fore, de, trans, super, semi, anti, mid,* and *under.* Four suffixes—*s/es, ed,* and *ing*—account for 65 percent of the suffixed words. Add *ly, er/or, ion/tion, ible/able, al, y, ness, ity,* and *ment,* and you account for 87 percent of the words. The remaining suffixes were *er/est, ic, ous, en, ive, ful,* and *less.*

Because White, Sowell, and Yanagihara (1989) were looking at prefixes and suffixes only from the standpoint of helping with the meaning part of big words, they did not include in their count "unpeelable" prefixes and suffixes such as the *con* in *conform* and the *ture* in *signature*. Although these prefixes and suffixes would not help students figure out the meaning of *conform* or *signature*, they are consistent spelling chunks, and noticing this pattern could help students spell words that begin with *con* and end with *ture*. The Prefixes, Suffixes, and Chunks chart shows the word parts taught in this chapter along with the key words.

Prefixes, Suffixes, and Chunks with Key Words			
Word part	**Key word**	**Change in meaning or how used**	**Type**
Prefixes			
anti	antibiotics	against or opposed to	prefix
com/con	complete composition command competition conclude continue confidence confident	with or together	unpeelable prefix

Word part	Key word	Change in meaning or how used	Type
de	defend defense defensive destroy destruction design defective	down or away	unpeelable prefix
de	delicious		chunk
dis	disappear dishonest	opposite	prefix
dis	discovery		chunk
en	encourage	make or give	prefix
en	entertain		chunk
ex	explode explosion explosive exports exploration excitement	out or away from	unpeelable prefix
im	impossible	opposite	prefix
im	immigrant impression impressive	in	prefix
im	important		chunk
in	incorrect invisible independent	opposite	prefix
in	indent	in	prefix
in	inventor inspector		chunk
inter	intersection	between or together	prefix
mis	misunderstood	wrongly or badly	prefix

Word part	Key word	Change in meaning or how used	Type
non	nonviolent	not or without	prefix
over	overweight	over or too much	prefix
per	performance		chunk
pre	preview prediction	before	prefix
pro	produce production promotion protective	for or forward	unpeelable prefix
re	remember		chunk
re	rebuild	again	prefix
re	recall	back	prefix
trans	transfer	across	unpeelable prefix
un	unhappily unbelievable	not or opposite	prefix
under	underground	under or less	prefix
Suffixes			
able	valuable unbelievable acceptable	able to do or having	suffix
al	equal		chunk
al	magical	adjective	suffix
ance	performance	noun	suffix
en	strengthen weaken	make or give	suffix
en	forgotten		chunk
ence	confidence	noun	suffix
ent	different confident independent nonviolent	adjective	suffix

Word part	Key word	Change in meaning or how used	Type
er	swimmer	person or thing	suffix
er	hotter	more	suffix
est	coolest	most	suffix
ful	beautiful	much or full of	suffix
ian	musician	person	suffix
ible	impossible invisible		chunk
ible	flexible	able to	suffix
ic	politics antibiotics		chunk
ify	classify	to make	suffix
ion	impression explosion	noun	suffix
ist	artist	person	suffix
ive	protective defective sensitive effective creative defensive impressive explosive	adjective	suffix
less	hopeless	none or without	suffix
ly	unhappily	adverb	suffix
ment	agreement excitement	noun	suffix
ment	apartment		chunk
ness	happiness	noun	suffix
or	governor inventor inspector	person	suffix

Word part	Key word	Change in meaning or how used	Type
ous	dangerous mountainous	adjective	suffix
ous	enormous		chunk
tion	direction prediction competition action production promotion information identification composition destruction exploration intersection	noun	suffix
tion	nation		chunk
ture	adventure signature		chunk
y	sunny cloudy	adjective	suffix
y	mystery		chunk
y	discovery electricity	noun	suffix

The work of Henderson and his followers, most clearly laid out in *Words Their Way* (Bear, Invernizzi, Templeton, & Johnston, 2008), shows children progressing through a number of stages as they become fluent spellers. The final stage, and the one of most interest for big words, is *derivational relations* (formerly called *derivational constancy*). This is the stage at which children notice the sophisticated patterns represented by the spelling of multisyllabic words and also the stage in which morphology plays a dominant role. Key words and activities in this chapter are appropriate for most students who are in the derivational relations stage.

In spite of the importance of morphological understandings to decoding, spelling, and meaning development, there is a lot of evidence that many older students lack much understanding of how words are related. Templeton (1992) reviews the research that he and colleagues have done regarding students' spelling development in the derivational constancy stage. In one set of studies, they set out to determine how aware middle-grade students are of the spelling–meaning connection. In interviews, students were asked if spelling made sense to them. They were also asked to decide if pairs of words such as *please/pleasant, limb/limber,* and *logic/logician* were related. Some of these pairs were shown to the students. For others, they did not see the pairs but heard the interviewer pronounce the words. They were also asked if the first *i* in words such as *define/definition* had the same sound in both words. If they replied the sounds were different, they were asked why the spelling didn't change to show that the sounds were different. Students gave a variety of responses including:

> "*Clinic* and *clinician* are related because of the spelling."

> "I doubt that *sign/signal* come from one another. I don't think the origin sounds the same."

> "*Origin* and *original* are not related because *original* means just something that is *original* and I don't know what the other one is and they don't sound alike." (p. 259)

There is evidence, however, that older students can be taught to notice morphological relationships and that this knowledge has a positive impact on spelling, decoding, and the acquisition of word meanings. Freyd and Baron (1982) investigated the extent to which readers' use of structural analysis is related to their reading ability. They found a strong relationship and concluded that skilled readers use structural analysis in three ways: to recognize known words more efficiently, to remember the meanings and spellings of partially learned words, and to figure out the meanings and pronunciations of new words. Baumann, Edwards, Font, Tereshinski, Kame'enui, and Olejnik (2002) demonstrated that students can be taught the meanings of select morphemic elements, and this morphemic knowledge enables them to infer the meanings of untaught words. McCutchen, Green, and Abbott (2008) examined the development of morphological knowledge among older elementary students and the relationship of their morphological knowledge to decoding. They found that morphological awareness continued to develop from fourth to sixth grades and that children's skill with morphology made a unique contribution to decoding ability. Nunes and Bryant (2006) conducted a series of studies in which fourth-graders received instruction in morphemes. The students who received the morphemic instruction made greater gains in spelling and vocabulary than students who did not receive such instruction.

Long words, like short words, are spelled by pattern. The patterns in long words are prefixes, suffixes, and predictable chunks. Once your students can spell some long words and learn how the parts of these longer words can be combined to help them spell other words, they are on their way to becoming excellent spellers.

Their writing will become much more vivid, precise, and vibrant as they become confident in their ability to spell the words they want to use to tell their story.

As with shorter words, words your students can spell quickly and automatically are the raw material for spelling hundreds of other words. The chart called 100 Big Key Words will provide that raw material. Add these words gradually to your word wall. Provide auditory and kinesthetic practice with these words by leading your students to cheer and write them. Then provide many opportunities for your students to use the chunks of these big words to spell other words. This chapter contains lessons you can use to teach these 100 words and—more importantly—the hundreds of other words the patterns in these words will enable them to spell.

100 Big Key Words				
acceptable	action	adventure	agreement	antibiotics
apartment	artist	beautiful	classify	cloudy
command	competition	complete	composition	conclude
confidence	confident	continue	coolest	creative
dangerous	defective	defend	defense	defensive
delicious	design	destroy	destruction	different
direction	disappear	discovery	dishonest	effective
electricity	encourage	enormous	entertain	equal
excitement	explode	exploration	explosion	explosive
exports	flexible	forgotten	governor	happiness
hopeless	hotter	identification	immigrant	important
impossible	impression	impressive	incorrect	indent
independent	information	inspector	interesting	intersection
inventor	invisible	magical	migrate	misunderstood
mountainous	musician	mystery	nation	nonviolent
offender	offense	overweight	performance	politics
prediction	preview	produce	production	promotion
protective	rebuild	recall	remember	sensitive
signature	strengthen	sunny	swimmer	transfer
unbelievable	underground	unhappily	valuable	weaken

Is 100 Words Enough for Older Students?

If you teach in the intermediate or middle grades, you may worry that 100 words—5 a week—is not enough words. But you need to think about these words not as individual words but as key words—anchor words for all the morphemic and spelling knowledge you are building. You do want all your students to learn to spell these words, but being able to spell them is not your ultimate goal. Your ultimate goal is that they can use these words to help them figure out the complex system of how big words in English work. Almost all big words are combinations of roots, prefixes, and suffixes. When these are combined, spelling and pronunciation changes often occur. If your students can spell these words and analyze and explain their components, they have the keys to unlock the meaning, spelling, and pronunciation of thousands of new words. These 100 words are enough to develop your students' confidence and skill as they encounter unfamiliar big words in all subjects throughout the school day.

• The First 5 Words

Begin your word wall with these five words:

> coolest   hotter   hopeless   beautiful   unhappily

Talk with your students about these words and the parts and spelling changes that make them up.

> *Coolest* is the word *cool* with suffix *est*—meaning "most" at the end. You know lots of words that can have *est* added to them to make them mean most.

Let students name some *est* words—*greatest, strongest, fastest*—and observe that the suffix *est* adds the meaning of most.

Continue to talk about the other words and have students name other words they know with the same parts and meaning. Use the word in a sentence if that clue is needed to clarify meaning.

> *Hotter* means "more hot." Remember that we double the *t* when we add a part that begins with a vowel. What are some other words you know that end in *er* in which *er* means more?

> *Hopeless* is the word *hope* with the suffix *less* added to it. The suffix *less* often means "none or without." If something is hopeless, there is no hope. When our quarterback was injured, we knew a state championship was hopeless. What are some other words you know where *less* means none or without? (*helpless, sleepless, worthless*)

Beautiful is the word *beauty* with the suffix *ful* added to it. The suffix *ful* often means "much or full of." If something is beautiful, it has much beauty. How do we spell *beauty?* Notice the spelling change *y* to *i* when *ful* is added. What are some other words you know where *ful* means much or full of?   (*hopeful, merciful, powerful*)

Unhappily is the word *happy* with the prefix *un* and the suffix *ly* added to it. The prefix *un* often changes a word to its opposite meaning. The suffix *ly* changes how a word is used. *Unhappily* means "not happily." Notice that the *y* at the end of *happy* changes to an *i* when *ly* is added. What are some other words you know where *un* means not or opposite? What are some other words you know that end in *ly?*

After helping your students notice the parts and spelling changes, get your students out of their seats and lead them to cheer for the words. Make your cheering rhythmic—with a slight pause between the word parts. Cheer for each word three times and say the word at the beginning and end of the cheer.

"coolest c-o-o-l---e-s-t; c-o-o-l---e-s-t; c-o-o-l---e-s-t; coolest"

"hotter h-o-t---t-e-r; h-o-t---t-e-r; h-o-t---t-e-r; hotter"

"unhappily u-n---h-a-p-p-i---l-y; u-n---h-a-p-p-i---l-y; u-n---h-a-p-p-i---l-y; unhappily"

"hopeless h-o-p-e---l-e-s-s; h-o-p-e---l-e-s-s; h-o-p-e---l-e-s-s; hopeless"

"beautiful b-e-a-u-t-i---f-u-l; b-e-a-u-t-i---f-u-l; b-e-a-u-t-i---f-u-l; beautiful"

Ask your students to sit down and lead them to write each word, talking again about the parts and the spelling changes.

coolest

hotter

unhappily

hopeless

beautiful

On the following day, ask your students to tell you about the words.

What are the parts in *hopeless?* What does the *less* mean? What words do you know that end in *less* and *less* means "without or none"?

What are the parts in *beautiful?* What spelling change do we need? What does the *ful* mean? What words do you know that end in *ful* and *ful* means "much or full of"?

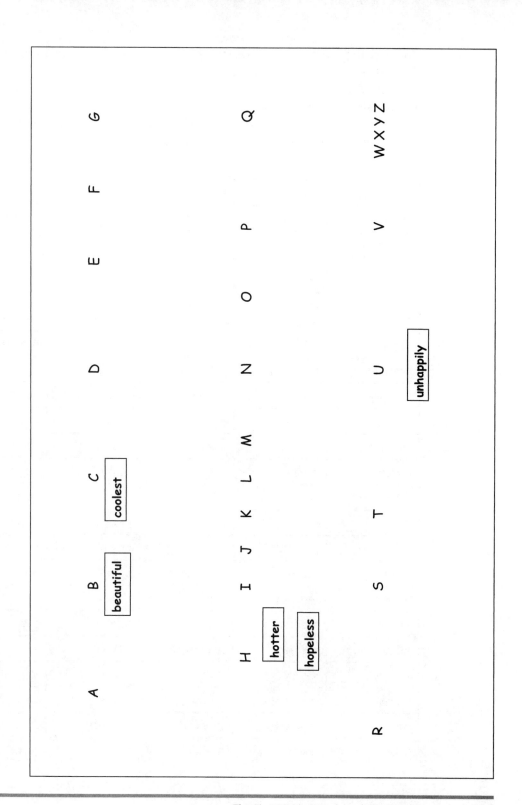

A B C D E F G

beautiful coolest

H I J K L M N O P Q

hotter

hopeless

R S T U V W X Y Z

unhappily

Continue to have students analyze the words *unhappily, hottest,* and *coolest.* Also lead the students to cheer and write the words again.

For the next several days, lead your students in a quick cheer of the word wall words and then have them spell words that combine these parts with words they can spell. Before you add the next five words, your students should confidently and quickly be spelling these words.

beauty	bigger	biggest	bravely	braver
bravest	brighter	brightest	brightly	careful
carefully	careless	carelessly	clearly	colder
coldest	darker	darkest	drier	driest
faster	fastest	fearful	fearfully	fearless
fearlessly	friendlier	friendliest	friendly	handful
happier	happiest	happily	harder	hardest
harmful	harmfully	harmless	harmlessly	helpful
helpfully	helpless	helplessly	homeless	hopeful
hopefully	hopelessly	joyful	joyfully	kinder
kindest	kindly	lately	later	latest
lawless	lighter	lightest	lightly	longer
longest	lower	lowest	nearer	nearest
nearly	older	oldest	painful	painfully
painless	painlessly	playful	playfully	prettier
prettiest	quicker	quickest	quickly	restful
restless	restlessly	richer	richest	richly
sadder	saddest	sadly	safely	safer
safest	sharper	sharpest	sharply	shorter
shortest	shortly	skillful	skillfully	slightly
slower	slowest	slowly	smaller	smallest
smarter	smartest	stronger	strongest	strongly
taller	tallest	thankful	thankfully	thankless

thanklessly	thicker	thickest	thinner	thinnest
unfair	unfairly	unfriendly	unfriendlier	unfriendliest
unhappier	unhappy	unjust	unjustly	unkind
unkindly	unlawful	unlock	unpack	unsafe
unsafely	useful	usefully	useless	uselessly

● The Next 5 Words

The first 5 words were chosen so that you could quickly impress your students with the power of patterns in big words. From these 5 words, they should be able to spell more than 100 additional words. Not all the words you add to the wall will be as generative but all the words will help your students add many words—with the final number over 1,000 when all 100 big words are on the wall and their patterns are being used by your students.

The next five words to add to your wall are:

swimmer   artist   remember   rebuild   recall

As you add these words to your wall, talk with your students about these words and the parts and spelling changes that make them up. Use the words in a sentence if that clue is needed to clarify meaning.

A *swimmer* is a person or animal that swims. The suffix *er* often means "the person or thing that does something." We double the *m* when adding *er*. What other words do you know in which *er* means a person or thing that does something?

An *artist* is a person who creates *art*. The suffix *ist* often means "the person who does something." What other words do you know in which *ist* means a person who does something?

When we *rebuild* something, we build it again. The prefix *re* often means "again." Sometimes, the prefix *re* means "back." When a company *recalls* something, they call it back because there is some kind of problem. What are some other words you know in which *re* means back or again?

Many words begin with the chunk *re* but *re* does not mean "back or again." *Remember* is an example of a word that begins with *re* but the *re* does not add or change the meaning of the word.

When you have talked with your students about these words and added them to the word wall, ask your students to stand up and then lead them to cheer for the words. Make your cheering rhythmic—with a slight pause between the word parts. Cheer for each word three times and say the word at the beginning and end of the cheer.

"recall r-e---c-a-l-l; r-e---c-a-l-l; r-e---c-a-l-l; recall"

"rebuild r-e---b-u-i-l-d; r-e---b-u-i-l-d; r-e---b-u-i-l-d; rebuild"

"remember r-e-m-e-m-b-e-r; r-e-m-e-m-b-e-r; r-e-m-e-m-b-e-r; remember

"artist a-r-t---i-s-t; a-r-t---i-s-t; a-r-t---i-s-t; artist"

"swimmer s-w-i-m---m-e-r; s-w-i-m---m-e-r; s-w-i-m---m-e-r; swimmer"

Ask your students sit down and lead them to write each word, talking again about the parts and the spelling changes.

recall

rebuild

remember

artist

swimmer

On the following day, ask your students to tell you about the words.

What are the parts in *recall* and *rebuild?* What does *re* sometimes mean? What words do you know where *re* means "back or again"?

Continue to have your students explain and give similar words for *artist* and *swimmer*. Lead the students to cheer and write these five new words again. For the next several days, choose any 5 of the 10 words on your wall and lead your students in a quick cheer for these words. Then have students spell some of the words that can be spelled using words they know and word wall words. Before you add the next 5 words, your students should confidently and quickly be spelling these words:

baker	banker	batter	build	builder
bumper	buyer	catcher	cracker	cyclist
dentist	diver	driver	drummer	farmer
fighter	florist	heater	leader	locker

pitcher	player	printer	rapper	react
rebound	record	recorder	refill	reform
reformer	refund	relay	remark	remind
reminder	remove	rename	repaint	repair
repeat	replace	reprint	report	reporter
require	reread	restore	retell	retire
retreat	return	rewrite	rider	robber
skater	slippers	teacher	tourist	typist
worker	writer	zipper		

You're the Expert!

I may be the expert on spelling but you are the expert on your students. I have tried to include only words most intermediate-aged children would have in their listening vocabularies. Thus, I didn't include words such as *regret* or *retrace* that your students might not connect to any meaning. But remember, you are the expert on your kids. Omit from all my lists words your students cannot connect meanings to and add any you think they might know. Look at the lists throughout the chapter as starting points for customizing your own list of words.

To help them think about the meaning of *re* in some words, give them a list of words that begin with *re*. Have them work in groups to sort them into three columns:

re meaning back	*re* meaning again	*re* spelling chunk
recall	rebuild	remember

● Add 5 More Words

If you and your students are keeping count, the 10 words on your word wall have now increased your spelling power to almost 200 words! As you add the next 5 words, talk with your students about the suffixes *al* and *ous* and how they change the way a word can be used in a sentence.

equal   magical   dangerous   mountainous   enormous

The suffixes *al* and *ous* change a word into a describing word or adjective. When something happens as if by magic, we say it is *magical*. When we are in danger, we say it is a *dangerous* situation. A place with lots of mountains is *mountainous*. Sometimes, as in the words *equal* and *enormous*, *al* and *ous* are just spelling chunks and do not affect the word's meaning.

Ask the students to share any words they know that end in *al* or *ous* and how these suffixes change words into describing words (*poisonous*, *nervous*, *musical*, *personal*).

When you have talked with your students about these words and added them to the word wall, get your students out of their seats and lead them to cheer for the words. Remember to cheer for each word three times and make your cheering rhythmic—with a slight pause between the word parts.

"equal e-q-u-a-l; e-q-u-a-l; e-q-u-a-l; equal"

"magical m-a-g-i-c---a-l; m-a-g-i-c---a-l; m-a-g-i-c---a-l; magical"

"dangerous d-a-n-g-e-r---o-u-s; d-a-n-g-e-r---o-u-s; d-a-n-g-e-r---o-u-s; dangerous"

"mountainous m-o-u-n-t-a-i-n---o-u-s; m-o-u-n-t-a-i-n---o-u-s; m-o-u-n-t-a-i-n---o-u-s mountainous"

"enormous e-n-o-r-m-o-u-s; e-n-o-r-m-o-u-s; e-n-o-r-m-o-u-s; enormous"

Tell the children to sit down and lead them to write each word, talking again about the parts and the spelling changes.

equal

magical

dangerous

mountainous

enormous

On the following day, ask your students to tell you about the words.

How do the suffixes *ous* and *al* change some words they are added to?
Can you remember the other *ous* and *al* words we talked about?

Lead the students to cheer and write these five new words again.

For the next several days, choose any 5 of the 15 word wall words and lead your students in a quick cheer for these words.

Call out several words from this list and have your students explain what parts of the word wall words they will use to spell these words: Be sure to talk about spelling changes before students write the words. As students write words, ask them if *ous* and *al* are suffixes that change meaning or just spelling chunks.

danger	dangerously	enormously	equally	famous
famously	final	finally	global	globally
joyous	joyously	local	locally	loyal
loyally	magic	magically	medal	metal
monstrous	mountain	mural	normal	normally
pedal	personal	personally	removal	rental
rival	royal	royally	rural	total
totally	tribal	unequal	vital	vitally

● Add 5 More Words

The next five words to add to your wall are:

sunny   cloudy   mystery   discovery   electricity

All these words end in *y*. For *sunny* and *cloudy,* the suffix *y* changes these words into describing words or adjectives. When the sun is out, we say it is a *sunny* day. When there are lots of clouds in the sky, we say it is a *cloudy* day. The *y* at the end of *discovery* and *electricity* changes the root words into nouns. Something you discover is called a *discovery; electricity* is what powers electric appliances. The *y* at the end of *mystery* is a spelling chunk and does not add any meaning to the word.

Ask your students to think of other words that end in *y* and help them decide if the *y* is a suffix that changes the word into an adjective (*rainy, windy*), a noun (*security, delivery*), or just a spelling chunk (*library, community*).

When you have talked about all five words, lead your students to cheer these words.

"sunny s-u-n---n-y; s-u-n---n-y; s-u-n---n-y; sunny"

"cloudy c-l-o-u-d---y; c-l-o-u-d---y; c-l-o-u-d---y; cloudy"

"electricity e-l-e-c-t-r-i-c---i-t-y; e-l-e-c-t-r-i-c---i-t-y; e-l-e-c-t-r-i-c---i-t-y; electricity"

"discovery d-i-s-c-o-v-e-r---y; d-i-s-c-o-v-e-r---y; d-i-s-c-o-v-e-r---y; discovery"

"mystery m-y-s-t-e-r-y; m-y-s-t-e-r-y; m-y-s-t-e-r-y; mystery"

Then lead them to write each word, talking again about the parts and the spelling changes.

sunny

cloudy

electricity

discovery

mystery

On the following day, ask your students to tell you about the words.

How does the suffix *y* change some words? Can you remember the other words that end in *y* we talked about?

Lead the students to cheer and write these five new words again.

For the next several days, choose any 5 of the 20 words on the wall and lead your students in a quick cheer for these 5 words. Call out words from this list and have your students explain what parts of the word wall words they will use to spell these words. Be sure to talk about spelling changes before students write the words. As students write words, ask them to explain how *y* changes meaning or is just a spelling chunk.

bakery	bravery	bumpier	bumpiest	bumpy
chillier	chilliest	chilly	cloudier	cloudiest
cloudless	curlier	curliest	curly	dirtier
dirtiest	dirty	discover	drippy	dusty
electric	electrical	equality	foggier	foggiest
foggy	funnier	funniest	grassy	jumpy

loyalty	lumpy	mysterious	penny	puppy
rainier	rainiest	rainy	reality	recover
recovery	risky	royalty	runny	rusty
skinnier	skinniest	skinny	slippery	sunnier
sunniest	uncover	vitality	windier	windiest
windy				

● Add 5 More Words

The next five words to add to your wall are:

> disappear   dishonest   agreement   excitement   apartment

Sometimes the prefix *dis* turns a word into its opposite meaning. The opposite of *appear* is *disappear*. The opposite of *dishonest* is *honest*. Sometimes, as in the word *discovery* we already have on our word wall, *dis* is just a spelling chunk. The suffix *ment* can change a root word into a noun. When you agree to something, you have an *agreement*. When you are excited about something, you feel *excitement*. Other times, as in *apartment*, *ment* is just a spelling chunk.

Ask your students to name some other words in which the *dis* turns a word into its opposite meaning (*disobey, displease*) and some other words in which *ment* is added and the root word is changed into a noun (*enjoyment, movement*).

When you have talked about all five words, lead your students to cheer these words.

> "dishonest d-i-s---h-o-n-e-s-t; d-i-s---h-o-n-e-s-t; d-i-s---h-o-n-e-s-t; dishonest"

> "disappear d-i-s---a-p-p-e-a-r; d-i-s---a-p-p-e-a-r; d-i-s---a-p-p-e-a-r; disappear"

> "excitement e-x-c-i-t-e---m-e-n-t; e-x-c-i-t-e---m-e-n-t; e-x-c-i-t-e---m-e-n-t; excitement"

> "agreement a-g-r-e-e---m-e-n-t; a-g-r-e-e---m-e-n-t; a-g-r-e-e---m-e-n-t; agreement"

> "apartment a-p-a-r-t-m-e-n-t; a-p-a-r-t-m-e-n-t; a-p-a-r-t-m-e-n-t; apartment"

Then lead them to write each word, talking again about the parts and the spelling changes.

dishonest

disappear

excitement

agreement

apartment

On the following day, ask your students to tell you about the words.

How does the prefix *dis* sometimes change words? Can you remember the other words in which *dis* changes a word to the opposite? How does *ment* change root words? Can you remember other words where adding *ment* turns the root word into a noun?

Lead the students to cheer and write these five new words again.

For the next several days, choose 5 of the 25 words to review and have your students quickly cheer and write these 5 words. Then have them spell some other words that can be spelled using the parts of the word wall words. Be sure to talk about spelling changes before any words are written. Have students tell you in which words *dis* has the opposite meaning and *ment* changes a word into a noun.

agree	appear	basement	disagree	disagreement
disarm	discount	disgrace	dishonestly	dishonesty
dislike	disloyal	disloyalty	dismiss	display
displease	disposal	dispose	disprove	distant
distrust	distrustful	excited	excitedly	exciting
honest	honestly	honesty	moment	movement
pavement	payment	placement	reappear	repayment
replacement	shipment	statement	torment	treatment

Word Parts Taught in These 25 Words

If your students can spell all 25 words, they are on their way to conquering big words. In addition to being able to spell these words, they are building a lot of morphological sophistication. This chart shows what they should understand about how prefixes and suffixes change meaning or how a word can be used in a sentence. Spelling changes taught in previous chapters are reviewed. Word parts indicated as chunks help students pronounce and spell words but do not help develop meaning.

Word part	Key word	Change in meaning or how used	Spelling change	Type
est	coolest	most		suffix
er	hotter	more	doubling	suffix
less	hopeless	none or without		suffix
ful	beautiful	much or full of	y-i	suffix
un	unhappily	not or opposite	y-i	prefix
ly	unhappily	adverb	y-i	suffix
er	swimmer	person or thing	doubling	suffix
ist	artist	person		suffix
re	remember			chunk
re	rebuild	again		prefix
re	recall	back		prefix
al	equal			chunk
al	magical	adjective		suffix
ous	dangerous mountainous	adjective		suffix
ous	enormous			chunk
y	sunny	adjective	doubling	suffix
y	cloudy	adjective		suffix
y	mystery			chunk

Word part	Key word	Change in meaning or how used	Spelling change	Type
y	discovery electricity	noun		suffix
dis	disappear dishonest	opposite		prefix
dis	discovery			chunk
ment	excitement agreement	noun		suffix
ment	apartment			chunk

Review, Consolidate, Celebrate!

Like magic, your 25 words have now empowered your students to spell over 300 words. Take a week off from adding words and use the following games and activities to review the word wall words and the words they generate. In this section, you will find activities and games you can use for review and during the weeks you are adding words.

● Be a Mind Reader

Lead your students in several rounds of Be a Mind Reader to focus on the spelling and parts of the word wall words. In this game, you think of a word on the wall and then give five clues to that word. Choose a word and write it on a scrap of paper but do not let the students see what word you have written. Have your students number their papers from 1 to 5 and tell them that you are going to see who can read your mind and figure out which of the words on the wall you are thinking of and have written on your paper. Tell them you will give five clues. By the fifth clue, everyone should guess your word, but if they read your mind, they might get it before the fifth clue.

For your first clue, always give the same clue: "It's one of the words on the wall." Tell your students to write next to number 1 the word they think it might be. Each succeeding clue should narrow down what it can be until by clue 5 there is only one possible word. As you give clues, students write the word they believe it is next to each number. If succeeding clues confirm the word a student has written next to one number, the student writes that word again by the next number. If succeeding clues eliminate the word, the students choose a new word that fits all

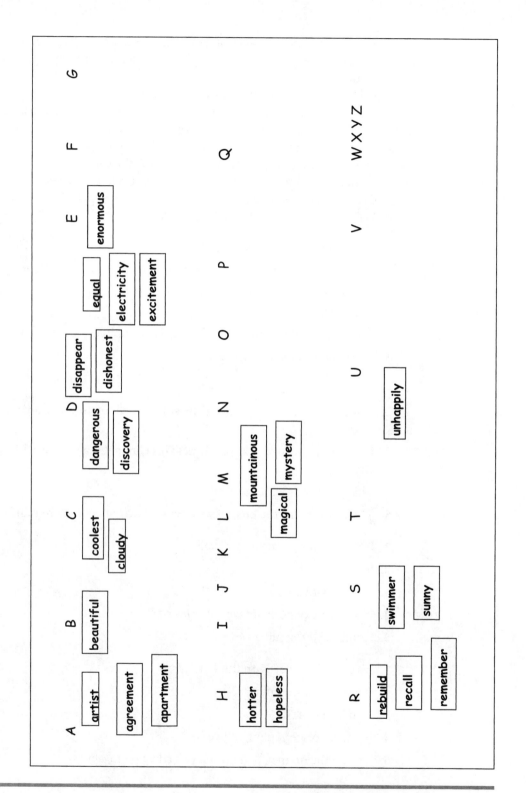

A
artist
agreement
apartment

B
beautiful

C
coolest
cloudy

D
disappear
dangerous
discovery
dishonest

E
enormous
equal
electricity
excitement

F

G

H
hotter
hopeless

I

J

K

L
mountainous
magical
mystery

M

N

O

P

Q

R
rebuild
recall
remember

S
swimmer
sunny

T

U
unhappily

V

W X Y Z

the clues. Clues may include any features of the word you want students to notice. (It has a prefix. It does not have a suffix. It has a spelling change. It begins with *re*. It has nine letters.)

After clue 5, show students the word you wrote on your scratch paper and say, "I know you all have the word next to number 5 but who has it next to number 4? 3? 2? 1?" All students who guessed the word on line 1 are the winners. If no one guessed it on line 1, the winners are everyone who guessed it on line 2. In the unlikely event that no one guessed it on line 1 or 2, the winners are everyone who guessed it on line 3. Once you have your winners, check their papers to make sure the word is spelled correctly every time. If the word is not spelled correctly, they do not win! Here are some examples to get you started.

1. It's one of the words on the wall.
2. It starts with a prefix. (The students eliminate any word without a prefix.)
3. The prefix can turn a word into its opposite meaning. (The *re* words are eliminated.)
4. This word begins with the prefix *dis*. (This eliminates *unhappily*.)
5. The word means "not honest."

1. It's one of the words on the wall.
2. It does not start with a prefix. (The students eliminate any word with a prefix.)
3. It does not have a spelling change. (This eliminates all words with spelling changes.)
4. This word ends with the prefix *y*.
5. The word means the kind of weather we have when it might rain.

1. It's one of the words on the wall.
2. It has nine letters.
3. It starts with a *d*.
4. It is not the opposite of *appear* or *honest*.
5. It ends with the suffix *ous*.

1. It's one of the words on the wall.
2. It has 9 or more letters.
3. It ends in *ment*.
4. It is not a place you might live.
5. It is not the noun you get when you add *ment* to *agree*.

After your students understand how to play Be a Mind Reader, put them in pairs and have them choose a word and write down the five clues they will give the class to see if the class can read their minds. Check their clues to be sure they work before letting them share their clues with the class.

● Ruler Tap

Ruler Tap is a simple activity but kids love it and it does help them review the words. Begin the game by calling out a word and tapping the ruler for several of the letters. When you stop tapping, call on a student to finish spelling the word out loud. If that student correctly finishes spelling the word, give the ruler to that student and let that student call out a word and tap some of the letters. That student calls on another student and if that student correctly finishes spelling the word, that student gets the ruler and the game continues!

● WORDO

WORDO is a variation of the ever-popular Bingo game. Your students will love it and won't even realize they are getting a lot of practice spelling the word wall words. To prepare for this game, make lots of copies of a 5 × 5 table. This WORDO grid will accommodate all 25 words from your wall. Write each word on an index card and have your students write each word in one of the squares. When they have finished, all your students will have the same 25 words—but they should have put them in different squares. Explain that the first person to have a row or column or diagonal covered will be the winner—but that each word must be spelled correctly. Give your students something to cover the words—Cheerios or other cereal make for a nutritious snack and easy cleanup. Whenever someone wins, everyone clears the WORDO card by eating the cereal! Shuffle your cards and call out one word at a time. When students shout "WORDO," check their sheets to make sure all the words were called and they have spelled all the words correctly before declaring them the winners! Shuffle your cards and let them play another round or two. You might let the winner become the next caller and you can play the winner's sheet. Your students will love watching their teacher lose!

Save your deck of 25 cards and add 5 cards to it as you add words to the wall. When you want to review word wall words for the rest of the year, you can give your students blank WORDO sheets and let them choose 25 words from the wall to write on their sheets. With only 25 words, you can't play for a "full card," but in the weeks to come, your students will be choosing 25 words from all the word wall words and you can vary the game by sometimes playing for a full card!

artist	agreement	mountainous	beautiful	coolest
cloudy	dangerous	equal	discovery	enormous
electricity	disappear	excitement	dishonest	unhappily
sunny	remember	swimmer	rebuild	hotter
recall	hopeless	magical	mystery	apartment

● What's My Rule?

What's My Rule? is a word-sorting game you can use to help your students sort the word wall words and generated words into patterns. For this game, choose and make a list of 100 words, including both word wall words and other words they should be able to spell. Put your students into trios (groups of three) and give each trio a copy of the list.

agree	appear	baker	bakery	banker
hotter	batter	bigger	biggest	bravely
coolest	bravery	bravest	artist	recall
brightly	builder	bumper	rebuild	bumpiest
bumpy	buyer	careful	carefully	careless
carelessly	catcher	hopeless	beautiful	monstrous
treatment	clearly	unhappy	unpack	disappear
replacement	curlier	curliest	honest	cyclist
darker	darkest	dentist	remember	enormous
rewrite	disagree	swimmer	discover	dangerous
dishonesty	dislike	harmful	display	displease
recover	unlock	disprove	mysterious	distrust

distrustful	diver	drier	hopeful	unhappily
driver	drummer	dusty	electric	electrical
recovery	magical	mountainous	exciting	famous
famously	harmless	faster	dishonest	fearful
fearfully	fearless	fearlessly	fighter	final
finally	florist	foggier	playful	personal
friendlier	friendliest	friendly	electricity	discovery
funniest	agreement	excitement	global	globally

Model how you play What's My Rule? by choosing some words that share a common feature and writing them on a large sheet of paper. Tell your students that you were following a secret rule you made up to decide which words to include and which not to include. After you write each list of words, call on volunteers to guess your rule. Here are some examples to get you started:

1. brightly carelessly famously fearfully finally fearlessly carefully globally unhappily bravely clearly
   - **What's my rule?** (Words that end in *ly*)

2. bravely bravery bravest
   - **What's my rule?** (Words with the root word *brave*)

3. careless carelessly hopeless harmless fearless fearlessly
   - **What's my rule?** (Words with the suffix *less*)

Appoint a recorder in each trio and give each recorder several large pieces of paper and a marker. As the trio decides on a group of words, the recorder should write the words large enough for the class to see. With a pencil, in small letters on the back, the recorder should write the rule. Give the trios 15 minutes to see how many word groups they can form. Be sure they understand they can use the words again in different groups. Circulate and give assistance as needed to be sure the children include all the words that follow the rule they decide on. After 15 minutes, have each trio choose one group they want to share with the class. Assemble the class so that everyone can see the words that different trios have chosen. Let each trio read the words in one of their groups and call on volunteers to guess their rule.

● Odd Man Out

Odd Man Out is based on the game Odd Word Out described by Rasinski, Padak, Newton, and Newton (2008). Create sets of four words in which three share the same feature and one is the "odd man out." Have students work in pairs or trios to decide which word doesn't fit and why. When they understand how this game works, let the partners or trios create some for the other class members to solve. Here are some examples to get you started:

1. writer harder swimmer rapper

   The odd man out is _____ because _____.

   (*harder* because it is not a person)

2. unhappy unfair unhappily until

   The odd man out is _____ because _____.

   (*until* because *until* is not the opposite of *til*)

3. refill reformer reporter reminder

   The odd man out is _____ because _____.

   (*refill* because it does not end in *er*)

4. rental mural normal final

   The odd man out is _____ because _____.

   (*rental* because the *al* is a suffix added to *rent*; in other words, *al* is just a spelling chunk)

5. distrust distant disarm disagree

   The odd man out is _____ because _____.

   (*distant* because *dis* does not make *distant* the opposite of *tant*)

● Analogies

Have your students work in pairs or trios to solve these analogies and then make some of their own for the class to solve. When they have decided which word goes in the blank, have them make a sentence that shows the meanings of the two words. When they understand how analogies work, have them work in pairs or trios to create some for their classmates to solve.

1. Braver is to _____ as taller is to tallest.

   Sentence _____

   (I am braver than my little brother but my big sister is the bravest person I know.)

2. Handful is to _____ as armful is to arm.

Sentence _____

(I ate a handful of Red Hots and my hand is all red.)

3. Zip is to _____ as trap is to trapper.

Sentence _____

(I can't zip my jacket because the zipper is broken.)

4. Final is to _____ as normal is to normally.

Sentence _____

(I finally got a basket in the final game of the season.)

5. Pay is to _____ as place is to replacement.

Sentence _____

(My dad agreed to pay for the game but I had to make a $1.00 repayment to him out of my allowance every week.)

● Sentence Challenge

Challenge your students to write one sensible sentence that uses as many word wall words as they can. Let the class decide who has the best sentence.

> The enormous dog was dangerous.
>
> The artist lived in a beautiful, sunny apartment in the mountainous part of France.
>
> On a cloudy day, the swimmer disappeared in the dangerous water.

Spelling Skills Only Help if Students Use Them When They Write!

The only reason your students need to learn how to spell words is to enable them to write fluently and well. If they learn to spell words during your spelling practice but do not spell them correctly when writing, your spelling practice is wasted. Provide practice spelling the word wall words as they write sentences containing two or more of the words. When they are writing throughout the day, remind them to use the word wall and hold them accountable for spelling word wall words correctly in everything they write.

The Second 25 Big Words and Their Parts

 ● Add 5 More Words

The next five words to add to your wall are:

direction   prediction   competition   action   nation

Help your students to notice that all five words end in *tion* and that except for *nation,* the *tion* adds meaning to the words by changing base words into nouns.

> When you direct somebody, you give them *directions* about what to do or where to go. When you predict something is going to happen, you have made a *prediction*. When you compete in a race or other activity, you are in the *competition*. The way that you act is your *action*. In nation, the *tion* is just a spelling chunk and does not add any meaning to a root word.

> Lead your students to cheer the words:

> "nation n-a-t-i-o-n; n-a-t-i-o-n; n-a-t-i-o-n; nation"

> "action a-c-t---i-o-n; a-c-t---i-o-n; a-c-t---i-o-n; action"

> "prediction p-r-e-d-i-c-t---i-o-n; p-r-e-d-i-c-t---i-o-n; p-r-e-d-i-c-t---i-o-n; prediction"

> "direction d-i-r-e-c-t---i-o-n; d-i-r-e-c-t---i-o-n; d-i-r-e-c-t---i-o-n; direction"

> "competition c-o-m-p-e-t-i---t-i-o-n; c-o-m-p-e-t-i---t-i-o-n; c-o-m-p-e-t-i---t-i-o-n; competition"

Then lead them to write each word, talking again about the parts and the spelling changes.

> nation
>
> action
>
> prediction
>
> direction
>
> competition

On the following day, ask your students to explain to you how *tion* affects the meaning of some words, and lead them again to cheer and write the new *tion* words.

For the next several days, choose any five words you want to review and have your students quickly cheer and write these words. Then have them spell some other words that can be spelled using the parts of the word wall words. Be sure to talk about spelling changes before any words are written. Have students tell you in which words *tion* changes a word into a noun.

addition	additional	caption	compete	direct
donation	emotion	emotional	fraction	location
lotion	mention	motion	motionless	national
nationally	option	optional	portion	potion
predict	question	quotation	reaction	rotation
station	subtraction	taxation	traction	unemotional
vacation	vibration			

● Add 5 More Words

The next five words to add to your wall are:

politics   musician   valuable   acceptable   unbelievable

Talk with your students about word parts, meaning, and spelling changes.

Politics is a root word without any prefixes or suffixes. *Politics* is a word we use when we talk about government and the people who are in government.

A *musician* makes music. The suffix *ian* sometimes means the person who does something. Can you think of other words that end in *ian* and means that person is someone who does something? (magician, beautician)

Valuable, acceptable, and *unbelievable* all end with the suffix *able,* which means "able to do" or "having something." Something that is *valuable* has a lot of value. Something you can accept is *acceptable. Unbelievable* is the opposite of *believable.* If something is *unbelievable,* you can't believe it is true. When the suffix *able* is added to words that end in *e,* like *value* and *believe,* the *e* is dropped. Can you think of other words that end in *able* and mean able to do or having something? (*dependable, lovable*)

Lead your students to cheer the words:

"politics p-o-l-i-t-i-c-s; p-o-l-i-t-i-c-s; p-o-l-i-t-i-c-s; politics"

"musician m-u-s-i-c---i-a-n; m-u-s-i-c---i-a-n; m-u-s-i-c---i-a-n; musician"

"valuable v-a-l-u---a-b-l-e; v-a-l-u---a-b-l-e; v-a-l-u---a-b-l-e; valuable"

"acceptable a-c-c-e-p-t---a-b-l-e; a-c-c-e-p-t---a-b-l-e; a-c-c-e-p-t---a-b-l-e; acceptable"

"unbelievable u-n---b-e-l-i-e-v---a-b-l-e; u-n---b-e-l-i-e-v---a-b-l-e; u-n---b-e-l-i-e-v---a-b-l-e; unbelievable"

Then lead them to write each word, talking again about the parts and the spelling changes.

politics

musician

valuable

acceptable

unbelievable

On the following day, have students explain to you how *able* and *ian* affect the meaning of some words and lead them again to cheer and write the new words.

For the next several days, choose any 5 of the 35 words and have your students quickly cheer and write these words. Then have them spell other words that can be spelled using the parts of the word wall words and other words they can spell. Be sure to talk about spelling changes before any words are written and how word parts change the meaning of the root word.

accept	agreeable	agreeably	beautician	believable
believer	curable	disagreeable	disagreeably	electrician
excitable	lovable	magician	movable	music
musical	musically	political	politically	politician
portable	predictable	questionable	renewable	reusable
taxable	trainable	treatable	unacceptable	unbearable
unbeatable	unlikable	unlovable	unpredictable	unpredictably
unquestionable	untreatable	unusable	unworkable	usable
value	washable	workable		

● Add 5 More Words

The next five words to add to your wall are:

strengthen   weaken   forgotten   encourage   entertain

Talk with your students about word parts, meaning, and spelling changes.

En is a suffix at the end of some words and a prefix at the beginning of other words. Sometimes, *en* is just a spelling chunk. In *strengthen* and *weaken,* the suffix *en* means "to make or give." When you *strengthen* something, you give it strength or make it strong. When you *weaken* something, you make it weak. In *forgotten,* the *en* is just a spelling chunk. We double the *t* when we add *en* to forgot.

At the beginning of the word, *en* can also mean "to make or give." When you *encourage* someone to do something, you are trying to give them *courage.* The *en* in *entertain* is just a spelling chunk.

Lead your students to cheer the words:

"weaken w-e-a-k---e-n; w-e-a-k---e-n; w-e-a-k---e-n; weaken"

"strengthen s-t-r-e-n-g-t-h---e-n; s-t-r-e-n-g-t-h---e-n; s-t-r-e-n-g-t-h---e-n; strengthen"

"forgotten f-o-r-g-o-t-t-e-n; f-o-r-g-o-t-t-e-n; f-o-r-g-o-t-t-e-n; forgotten"

"encourage e-n---c-o-u-r-a-g-e; e-n---c-o-u-r-a-g-e; e-n---c-o-u-r-a-g-e; encourage"

"entertain e-n-t-e-r-t-a-i-n; e-n-t-e-r-t-a-i-n; e-n-t-e-r-t-a-i-n; entertain"

Then lead them to write each word, talking again about the parts and the spelling changes.

weaken

strengthen

forgotten

encourage

entertain

On the following day, ask your students to explain to you how *en* affects the meaning of some words and lead them again to cheer and write the new words.

For the next several days, choose any 5 of the 40 words and have your students quickly cheer and write these words. Then have them spell some other words that can be spelled using the parts of the word wall words and other words they can spell. Be sure to talk about spelling changes before any words are written and how word parts change the meaning of the root word.

beaten	bitten	broken	courage	darken
discourage	discouragement	enact	enchanted	encouragement
endanger	endure	enflame	engage	engagement
enjoyable	enjoyment	enrage	enrich	enrichment
ensure	enter	entire	entirely	frighten
frozen	given	golden	harden	hidden
lengthen	lighten	sharpen	spoken	stolen
taken	tighten	unbeaten	unbroken	unenjoyable
weakly	wooden	written		

● Add 5 More Words

The next five words to add to your wall are:

happiness   important   impossible   immigrant   migrate

Talk with your students about word parts, meaning, and spelling changes.

> *Ness* is a suffix that changes a word into a noun. When you are happy, you feel the emotion of *happiness*. What emotion do you feel when you are sad? When someone is kind to you, you appreciate their *kindness*. When they are friendly, you appreciate their *friendliness*.

> The prefix *im* can have two meanings. Sometimes, *im* changes a word to its opposite meaning. The opposite of *possible* is *impossible*. What is the opposite of *perfect*? What is the opposite of *patient*?

> Sometimes *im* can have the meaning of "in." *Immigrants* are people who come or migrate into this country. Do any of you have a relative who was an *immigrant*? What countries did they migrate from? *Imports* are things we bring into this country from other country. If you buy something that says "Made in China," that means we *imported* that, or brought it in, from China.

> Sometimes, as in the word *important*, *im* is just a spelling chunk.

Lead your students to cheer the words:

"happiness h-a-p-p-i---n-e-s-s; h-a-p-p-i---n-e-s-s;
h-a-p-p-i---n-e-s-s; happiness"

"impossible i-m---p-o-s-s-i-b-l-e; i-m---p-o-s-s-i-b-l-e;
i-m---p-o-s-s-i-b-l-e; impossible"

"migrate m-i-g-r-a-t-e; m-i-g-r-a-t-e; m-i-g-r-a-t-e; migrate "

"immigrant i-m---m-i-g-r-a-n-t; i-m---m-i-g-r-a-n-t;
i-m---m-i-g-r-a-n-t; immigrant"

"important i-m-p-o-r-t-a-n-t; i-m-p-o-r-t-a-n-t; i-m-p-o-r-t-a-n-t; important"

Then lead them to write each word, talking again about the parts and the spelling changes.

happiness

impossible

migrate

immigrant

important

After cheering for the words, have your students write each word.

On the following day, ask your students to explain to you the different meanings of *im* in *immigrants* and *impossible*. Lead them again to cheer and write the new words.

For the next several days, choose any 5 of the 45 words and have your students quickly cheer and write these words. Then have them spell some other words that can be spelled using the parts of the word wall words and other words they can spell. Be sure to talk about spelling changes before any words are written and how word parts change the meaning of the root word. For the words that begin with *im*, help your students decide if *im* changes a word to its opposite meaning, means "in," or is just a spelling chunk.

brighten	brightness	carelessness	darkness	fairness
fitness	forgiven	forgiveness	friendliness	goodness
illness	immigration	immovable	impeach	impeachment
implant	imports	impossibly	impress	improve
improvement	impure	kindness	madness	migrant
migration	possible	possibly	sadden	sadness
sharpness	sickness	thicken	thickness	unhappiness
unkindness	usefulness	uselessness	weakness	

● Add 5 More Words

The next five words to add to your wall are:

performance   interesting   incorrect   invisible   indent

Talk with your students about word parts, meaning, and spelling changes.

> The suffix *ance* changes a word into a noun. When you perform in a play or concert, you are part of the *performance*. To insure your car, you buy car *insurance.*

> Like *im,* the prefix *in* can have two meanings. Sometimes, *in* changes a word to its opposite meaning. The opposite of *correct* is *incorrect*. The opposite of *visible* is *invisible*. What is the opposite of *curable*? What is the opposite of *secure*?

> Sometimes *in* can have the meaning of "in." What do you do when you *indent* a paragraph? When it rains, we have *indoor* recess. Sometimes, as in the word *interesting, in* is just a spelling chunk.

Lead your students to cheer the words:

> "performance p-e-r-f-o-r-m---a-n-c-e; p-e-r-f-o-r-m---a-n-c-e; p-e-r-f-o-r-m---a-n-c-e; performance"

> "incorrect i-n---c-o-r-r-e-c-t; i-n---c-o-r-r-e-c-t; i-n---c-o-r-r-e-c-t; incorrect "

> "invisible i-n---v-i-s-i-b-l-e; i-n---v-i-s-i-b-l-e; i-n---v-i-s-i-b-l-e; invisible "

> "indent i-n---d-e-n-t; i-n---d-e-n-t; i-n---d-e-n-t; indent"

> "interesting i-n-t-e-r-e-s-t-i-n-g; i-n-t-e-r-e-s-t-i-n-g; i-n-t-e-r-e-s-t-i-n-g; interesting"

Then lead them to write each word, talking again about the parts and the spelling changes.

> performance
>
> incorrect
>
> invisible
>
> indent
>
> interesting

On the following day, have students explain to you the different meanings of *in* in *invisible, incorrect,* and *indent.* Lead them again to cheer and write the new words.

For the next several days, choose any 5 of the 50 words and have your students quickly cheer and write these words. Then have them spell some other words that can be spelled using the parts of the word wall words and other words they can spell. Be sure to talk about spelling changes before any words are written and how word parts change the meaning of the root word. For the words that begin with *im,* help your students decide if *im* changes a word to its opposite meaning, means "in," or is just a spelling chunk.

acceptance	appearance	clearance	correct	correction
correctly	disappearance	endurance	inaction	income
incorrectly	incurable	index	indirect	indirectly
indoors	inescapable	inland	inner	insane
insanity	insert	inside	insider	insurance
insure	intend	intent	intention	invent
invention	invisibility	invisibly	invitation	invite
perform	performer	uninsured	unintended	uninvited
visibility	visible	visibly		

Word Parts Taught in These 25 Words

Learning to spell and analyze these 25 words will help your students develop skill and confidence in reading, spelling, and building meaning for big words. This chart shows what they should understand about how prefixes and suffixes change meaning or how a word can be used in a sentence. Spelling changes taught previously are reviewed. Word parts indicated as chunks help students pronounce and spell words but do not help develop meaning.

Word part	Key word	Change in meaning or how used	Spelling change	Type
tion	direction prediction competition action	noun		suffix

Word part	Key word	Change in meaning or how used	Spelling change	Type
tion	nation			chunk
ic	politics			chunk
ian	musician	person		suffix
able	valuable unbelievable acceptable	able to do or having	drop e drop e	suffix
un	unbelievable	not or opposite		prefix
en	strengthen weaken	make or give		suffix
en	forgotten		double t	chunk
en	encourage	make or give		prefix
en	entertain			chunk
ness	happiness	noun	y to i	suffix
im	impossible	opposite		prefix
im	immigrant	in		prefix
im	important			chunk
in	incorrect invisible	opposite		prefix
in	indent	in		prefix
ible	impossible invisible			chunk
ance	performance	noun		suffix
per	performance			chunk

Review, Consolidate, Celebrate!

Like magic, your 50 words have now empowered your students to spell over 500 words! Take a week or two off from adding words and use the following games and activities to review the word wall words and the words they generate.

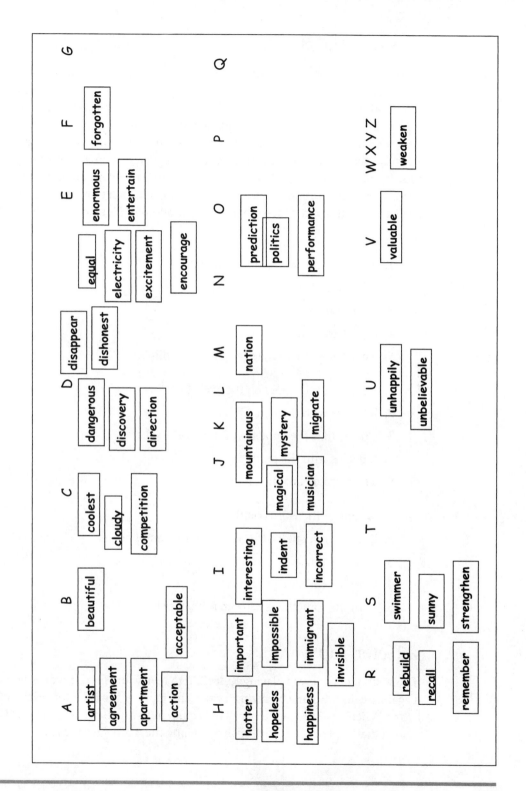

A
- artist
- agreement
- apartment
- action
- acceptable

B
- beautiful

C
- coolest
- cloudy
- competition

D
- dangerous
- discovery
- direction
- disappear
- dishonest

E
- equal
- enormous
- electricity
- excitement
- encourage
- entertain

F
- forgotten

G

H
- hotter
- hopeless
- happiness

I
- important
- impossible
- immigrant
- invisible
- interesting
- indent
- incorrect

J
- mountainous

K
- magical
- musician

L
- mystery
- migrate

M
- nation

N
- prediction
- politics
- performance

O

P

Q

R
- rebuild
- recall
- remember

S
- swimmer
- sunny
- strengthen

T

U
- unhappily
- unbelievable

V
- valuable

W X Y Z
- weaken

● Be a Mind Reader

Earlier in the chapter, you learned how to create Be a Mind Reader clues to focus your students' attention on the spelling and parts of the word wall words. With 50 words on the wall, it will be more difficult for anyone to guess the word on the first clue—although it will sometimes happen, surprising everyone, most of all the student who "read your mind." Remind your students that the winners are everyone who guessed the word after hearing the earliest clue—even if that is the third or fourth clue. Also remind them to continue writing the word on each line unless subsequent clues eliminate their guess. To win, the student must have the word spelled correctly every time—no ditto marks allowed! Here are some examples to get you started.

1. It's one of the words on the wall.
2. It has a suffix but not a prefix.
3. It has nine or more letters.
4. It ends with the suffix *ous*.
5. The root word is something you can climb.

1. It's one of the words on the wall.
2. It begins with the letter *i*.
3. The word is the opposite of the root word.
4. It begins with the prefix *in*.
5. The word means the opposite of visible.

1. It's one of the words on the wall.
2. It has a prefix that turns the word into an opposite.
3. It has a suffix.
4. It begins with the prefix *un*.
5. It means something you can not believe.

● Ruler Tap

If your students enjoyed playing Ruler Tap to review the first 25 words, you can use it again. Begin the game by saying a word and tapping the ruler for several of the letters. When you stop tapping, call on a student to finish spelling the word out loud. If that student correctly finishes spelling the word, give the ruler to that student and let that student say a word and tap some of the letters. That student calls on another student and if that student correctly finishes spelling the word, that student gets the ruler and the game continues!

● WORDO

Make sure your index card deck contains all 50 words. Let students choose any 25 to write on their WORDO sheet. Remind students to spell the word carefully because they win only if all the words covered are spelled correctly. When someone shouts "WORDO," check her or his sheet to make sure all the words were called and all the words are spelled correctly before declaring the student the winner! In addition to rows, columns, and diagonals, you can play for a "full card" if you have time. If you are not playing for a full card, shuffle your cards and play another round or two. Let the winner become the next caller and you play the winner's sheet. Maybe this time you will be the winner!

migrate	performance	mountainous	forgotten	direction
recall	invisible	nation	encourage	apartment
immigrant	impossible	interesting	dishonest	prediction
frighten	politics	action	rebuild	enjoy
indent	disappear	musician	agreement	strengthen

● What's My Rule?

Choose 100 words, including both word wall words and other words they should be able to spell. Put your students into trios (groups of three) and give each trio a copy of the list.

perform	appear	impatient	engagement	implant
incorrectly	invisibly	unbeaten	patiently	discourage
friendliness	question	indoors	unbroken	impatiently
forgiven	performer	performance	unhappily	bumpiest
impress	incorrect	interesting	carefully	portable
carelessly	invisible	happiness	happily	monstrous
national	questionable	unhappy	insane	disappearance
location	musician	impress	unhappiness	unbeatable
taxable	addition	dentist	agreeable	enormous
politician	nationally	swimmer	discover	dangerous
unpredictable	renewable	addition	reaction	electrician
musician	untreatable	disprove	mysterious	distrust
taxation	treatment	motionless	appearance	beautician
fraction	rotation	motion	electric	electrical
movable	magical	mountainous	exciting	famous
immigration	invader	vibration	dishonest	fearful
invade	invitation	fearlessly	invent	dishonest
insurance	thicken	unlovable	political	personal
forgiveness	kindness	friendly	electricity	discovery
discourage	immovable	excitement	invention	globally

Remind students how to play What's My Rule? by choosing some words that share a common feature and writing them on a large sheet of paper. After you write each list of words, call on volunteers to guess your rule. Here are some examples to get you started:

1. portable unbeatable questionable taxable agreeable renewable unlovable untreatable movable unpredictable immovable
   - **What's my rule?** (Words that end in *able*)

2. perform performance performer
   - **What's my rule?** (Words with the root word *perform*)

Appoint a recorder in each trio and give each recorder several large pieces of paper and a marker. As the trio decides on a group of words, the recorder should write the words large enough for the class to see. With a pencil, in small letters on the back, the recorder should write the rule. Give the trios 15 minutes to see how many word groups they can form. Be sure they understand they can use the words again in different groups. Circulate and give assistance as needed to be sure the children include all the words that follow the rule they decide on. After 15 minutes, have each trio choose one group they want to share with the class. Assemble the class so that everyone can see the words that different trios have chosen. Let each trio read the words in one of their groups and call on volunteers to guess their rule.

● Odd Man Out

Create sets of four words in which three share the same feature. The students work in pairs or trios to decide which word is the "odd man out." Here are some examples:

1. donation portion direction reaction

    The odd man out is _____ because _____.

    (*portion* because *tion* is just a spelling chunk)

2. music musician musical magic

    The odd man out is _____ because _____.

    (*magic* because magic is not related to music)

3. beautician artist cyclist weakest

    The odd man out is _____ because _____.

    (*weakest* because it is not a person)

4. stolen entire bitten hidden

    The odd man out is _____ because _____.

    (*entire* because it does not end in *en*)

5. migrant migration might immigrants

    The odd man out is _____ because _____.

    (*might* because *might* is not related to *migrate, migration,* and *immigrant*)

● Analogies

Have your students work in pairs or trios to solve these analogies and then make some of their own for the class to solve. When they have decided which word goes in the blank, have them make a sentence that shows the meanings of the two words. When they understand how analogies work, have them work in pairs or trios to create some for their classmates to solve.

1. Music is to _____ as magic is to magician.

   Sentence _____

   (A person who plays music is a musician.)

2. Kind is to _____ as fair is to fairness.

   Sentence _____

   (My grandma was kind to everyone and everyone noticed her kindness.)

3. Insurance is to _____ as endurance is to endure.

   Sentence _____

   (We needed to insure our new car and shopped around for the best insurance.)

4. Agreement is to _____ as improvement is to improve.

   Sentence _____

   (Everyone had to agree to follow the rules and sign the agreement.)

5. Predict is to _____ as act is to actions.

   Sentence _____

   (I predict we will win the game but my predictions are not always right.)

● Sentence Challenge

Challenge your students to write one sensible sentence that uses as many word wall words as they can. Let the class decide who has the best sentence.

   Our nation was built by immigrants who made the dangerous voyage here.

   How the musician disappeared before his performance was a mystery.

The Third 25 Big Words and Their Parts

 ● Add 5 More Words

The next five words to add to your wall are:

misunderstood   preview   intersection   underground   overweight

Talk with your students about word parts, meaning, and spelling changes.

The prefix *mis* often means "wrongly or badly." If you *misunderstood* something, you understood it wrongly. When you *misspell* a word, you spell it wrongly. If you *misbehave,* you behave badly.

The prefix *pre* sometimes means "before." When you see the *previews* for a movie, you are getting a chance to view part of the movie ahead of time and decide if you want to see the whole movie. A prefix comes before the rest of the word.

The prefix *inter* sometimes means "between or together." If an accident happened at the *intersection* of two streets, it happens between them—where the two streets come together. When we say pollution is an *international* problem, it is a problem that all nations face and countries must work together to solve.

The prefix *under* means "under or less." An *underground* train goes under the ground. The prefix *over* means "over or too much." If your luggage is *overweight,* it weighs too much and will cost more to ship it.

Lead your students to cheer the words:

"misunderstood m-i-s---u-n-d-e-r-s-t-o-o-d; m-i-s---u-n-d-e-r-s-t-o-o-d; m-i-s---u-n-d-e-r-s-t-o-o-d; misunderstood"

"preview p-r-e---v-i-e-w; p-r-e---v-i-e-w; p-r-e---v-i-e-w; preview"

"intersection i-n-t-e-r---s-e-c-t-i-o-n; i-n-t-e-r---s-e-c-t-i-o-n; i-n-t-e-r---s-e-c-t-i-o-n; intersection"

"underground u-n-d-e-r---g-r-o-u-n-d; u-n-d-e-r---g-r-o-u-n-d; u-n-d-e-r---g-r-o-u-n-d; underground"

"overweight o-v-e-r---w-e-i-g-h-t; o-v-e-r---w-e-i-g-h-t; o-v-e-r---w-e-i-g-h-t; overweight"

After cheering for the words, have your students write each word.

misunderstood

preview

intersection

underground

overweight

On the following day, ask your students to explain to you the meanings of the prefixes: *mis, pre, inter, under,* and *over* and give examples of words they know where the prefixes have these meanings. Lead them again to cheer and write the new words.

For the next several days, choose any 5 of the 55 words and have your students quickly cheer and write these words. Then have them spell some other words that can be spelled using the parts of the word wall words and other words they can spell. Be sure to talk about spelling changes before any words are written and how word parts change the meaning of the root word. For the words that begin with prefixes, help your students decide if these prefixes change a word's meaning or are just spelling chunks.

intercom	international	internationally	interpret	intersect
interstate	interview	interviewer	misbehave	mislead
misplace	misspell	mistake	mistaken	mistrust
mistrustful	misunderstand	misuse	overbuild	overcome
overcook	overdo	overeat	overexcited	overflow
overhand	overhead	overjoyed	overlap	overnight
overpass	overreact	overtake	overthrow	overview
prefer	preferable	preferably	prefix	preschool
present	pretend	pretest	prevent	preventable
prevention	review	reviewer	section	sectional
underage	underbrush	undercook	undercover	underhand
underpass	understand	understood	undertake	underweight
unpreventable	weightless	weightlessly		

● Add 5 More Words

The next five words to add to your wall are:

governor   inventor   inspector   flexible   antibiotics

Like *er, or* is a suffix that sometimes names a person or thing that does something. A *governor* is the head person in a state and governs the state. An *inventor* invents things. An *inspector* inspects things.

The suffix *ible,* like the suffix *able,* can mean "able to." If something is *flexible,* you can bend or flex it. (The *ible* in *impossible* and *invisible* is just a spelling chunk.)

The prefix *anti* can mean "opposed or against." *Antibiotics* are drugs that fight against infections. Why do you need antifreeze in your car if you live in a cold climate? What would if mean if you voted for the antiwar candidate?

When you have talked about all five words, lead your students to cheer and write these words.

"inspector i-n-s-p-e-c-t---o-r; i-n-s-p-e-c-t---o-r; i-n-s-p-e-c-t---o-r; inspector"

"governor g-o-v-e-r-n---o-r; g-o-v-e-r-n---o-r; g-o-v-e-r-n---o-r; governor"

"inventor i-n-v-e-n-t---o-r; i-n-v-e-n-t---o-r; i-n-v-e-n-t---o-r; inventor"

"flexible f-l-e-x---i-b-l-e; f-l-e-x---i-b-l-e; f-l-e-x---i-b-l-e; flexible"

"antibiotics a-n-t-i---b-i-o-t-i-c-s; a-n-t-i---b-i-o-t-i-c-s; a-n-t-i---b-i-o-t-i-c-s; antibiotics"

Then lead them to write each word, talking again about the parts and the spelling changes.

inspector
governor
inventor
flexible
antibiotics

On the following day, ask your students to explain how the suffixes *or* and *ible* affect the meanings of words. Then lead them to cheer and write these five words again.

For the next several days, choose five words you want to review and lead your students to cheer and write these five words. Then have the students use the word wall words to spell other words. Explain to students that although you can't hear the difference, the words that mean a person who does something will all be spelled with *or,* such as *inspector, inventor,* and *governor.* The words that mean able to do something will be spelled with *ible,* such as *flexible.*

actor	antibody	antifreeze	antitoxin	antiwar
competitor	creator	credible	director	donor
edible	editor	flexibility	flexibly	govern
government	governmental	incredible	inedible	inflexible
inspect	inspection	reflex	reinvent	respect
respectful	respond	responsibility	responsible	responsibly
sailor	sensible	sensibly	visitor	

● Add 5 More Words

The next five words to add to your wall are:

protective   defective   sensitive   creative   effective

Help the students to notice that all these words end in *ive* and that the *ive* changes the word into an adjective or describing word. Talk about spelling changes.

When we say a mother cat is *protective* of her baby kittens, we mean that she is trying to protect them. If you have to return something because it doesn't work, it has a defect and is *defective.* A person who is *sensitive* to others can sense how others are feeling and reacting. If you are a *creative* person, you can create new things and ideas. Something that works well is *effective* and has a good result or effect. You might read about a new drug being more effective than older drugs in treating patients with diabetes.

Lead your students to cheer the words:

"protective p-r-o-t-e-c-t---i-v-e; p-r-o-t-e-c-t---i-v-e;
p-r-o-t-e-c-t---i-v-e; protective"

"defective d-e-f-e-c-t---i-v-e; d-e-f-e-c-t---i-v-e;
d-e-f-e-c-t---i-v-e; defective"

"sensitive s-e-n-s-i-t---i-v-e; s-e-n-s-i-t---i-v-e; s-e-n-s-i-t---i-v-e; sensitive"

"creative c-r-e-a-t---i-v-e; c-r-e-a-t---i-v-e; c-r-e-a-t---i-v-e; creative"

"effective e-f-f-e-c-t---i-v-e; e-f-f-e-c-t---i-v-e; e-f-f-e-c-t---i-v-e; effective"

After cheering for the words, have your students write each word.

protective

defective

sensitive

creative

effective

On the following day, ask your students to explain to you how *ive* changes how words can be used in sentences. Lead them again to cheer and write the new words.

For the next several days, choose any 5 of the 65 words and have your students quickly cheer and write these words. Then have them spell some other words that can be spelled using the parts of the word wall words and other words they can spell. Be sure to talk about spelling changes before any words are written and how word parts change the meaning of the root word.

active	actively	captive	create	creation
creatively	creativity	defect	defection	effect
effectively	festive	inactive	inactively	ineffective
ineffectively	infect	infection	insensitive	insensitively
inventive	perfect	perfection	perfectionist	perfectly
preventive	protection	sense	sensitively	unprotected

● Add 5 More Words

The next five words to add to your wall are:

defend   defense   defensive   offense   offender

Contrast the words *defense* and *offense* by helping your students connect these words to football and then to other life situations. Help your students notice spelling changes.

A football team has a defense and an offense. The players on *defense* come in to *defend* their goal, to keep the other team from scoring. They form a *defensive* line in order to *defend* their goal. The players on *offense* move the ball down the line and try to score a goal. When we *defend* someone, we try to protect them.

When we *offend* someone, we say or do something rude or harmful to them. This rude behavior is *offensive*. *Offense* can also mean a crime. Robbery is a criminal *offense*. The person who commits the crime is called the *offender*.

When a verb such as *defend* or *offend* ends in *d,* the noun form usually ends in *se*. When EMTs respond to an emergency call, we call this a *response*.

Lead your students to cheer the words:

"defend d-e-f-e-n-d; d-e-f-e-n-d; d-e-f-e-n-d; defend"

"defense d-e-f-e-n-s-e; d-e-f-e-n-s-e; d-e-f-e-n-s-e; defense"

"defensive d-e-f-e-n-s---i-v-e; d-e-f-e-n-s---i-v-e;
d-e-f-e-n-s---i-v-e; defensive"

"offense o-f-f-e-n-s-e; o-f-f-e-n-s-e; o-f-f-e-n-s-e; offense"

"offender o-f-f-e-n-d---e-r; o-f-f-e-n-d---e-r; o-f-f-e-n-d---e-r; offender"

After cheering for the words, have your students write each word.

defend

defense

defensive

offense

offender

On the following day, ask your students to explain to you the relationship among *defend, defense,* and *defensive* and the spelling changes needed. Lead them again to cheer and write the new words.

For the next several days, choose any 5 of the 70 words and have your students quickly cheer and write these five words. Then have them spell other words that can be spelled using the parts of the word wall words and other words they can spell. Be sure to talk about spelling changes before any words are written and how word parts change the meaning of the root word.

defender	defenseless	defensively	expand	expansive
extend	extensive	extensively	inoffensive	intensive
intensively	offend	offensive	offensively	overextended
response	responsive	responsively	unresponsive	

● Add 5 More Words

The next five words to add to your wall are:

explode   explosion   explosive   impressive   impression

When something explodes, we say there was an *explosion*. Some gases can easily cause an *explosion* and we say these gases are *explosive*. When you impress someone with your clever thinking or an unlikely three-point shot, we say that it was *impressive* and your behavior made a great *impression* on everyone watching. For words that end in *de,* such as *explode,* the *d* changes to an *s* and the *e* is dropped when *ion* or *ive* is added. When you divide numbers, we call that *division*. When one country invades another country, we call that an *invasion*.

Lead your students to cheer the words:

"explode e-x-p-l-o-d-e; e-x-p-l-o-d-e; e-x-p-l-o-d-e; explode"

"explosion e-x-p-l-o---s-i-o-n; e-x-p-l-o---s-i-o-n;
e-x-p-l-o---s-i-o-n; explosion"

"explosive e-x-p-l-o---s-i-v-e; e-x-p-l-o---s-i-v-e;
e-x-p-l-o---s-i-v-e; explosive"

"impression i-m-p-r-e-s-s---i-o-n; i-m-p-r-e-s-s---i-o-n;
i-m-p-r-e-s-s---i-o-n; impression"

"impressive i-m-p-r-e-s-s---i-v-e; i-m-p-r-e-s-s---i-v-e;
i-m-p-r-e-s-s---i-v-e; impressive"

After cheering for the words, have your students write each word.

explode

explosive

explosion

impression

impressive

On the following day, have students explain the relationships and spelling changes for the words *explode, explosion,* and *explosive.* Lead them again to cheer and write the new words.

For the next several days, choose any 5 of the 75 words and have your students quickly cheer and write these 5 words. Then have them spell other words that can be spelled using the parts of the word wall words and other words they can spell. Be sure to talk about spelling changes before any words are written and how word parts change the meaning of the root word.

decide	decision	decisive	decisively	depress
depression	divide	divisible	division	divisive
expansion	expensive	express	expression	expressive
extension	implode	implosion	indecisive	indivisible
inexpensive	inexpressive	invade	invader	invasion
invasive	massive	passive		

● What Looks Right?

Some suffixes and chunks at the ends of words sound almost exactly alike but have different spellings. In the 75 key words your students have learned to spell, there are three pairs of suffixes—*er-or, tion-sion,* and *able-ible*—that share the same pronunciation. In order to determine which of these spellings is correct, your students need to develop a visual checking sense or use the dictionary to check the spelling. *What Looks Right?* is an activity to help your students develop a visual checking sense and to teach them how to use the dictionary to check the spelling of a word. To begin a *What Looks Right?* lesson, create two columns headed by two words that sound alike at the end but are spelled differently. Have your students write the same words in columns on their papers.

direction   explosion

Ask your students to pronounce and spell the words and lead them to realize that the words sound almost exactly the same at the end but have a different spelling. Highlight or underline the *tion* in *direction* and the *sion* in *explosion* and have them do the same on their papers. Tell them that there are many words that end like *direction* and *explosion* and that you can't tell just by saying the words which spelling is correct. Next, say a word that ends in *sion* and *tion* and write it both ways, saying, "If the word is spelled like *direction*, it will be - - - t-i-o-n. If it is spelled like *explosion*, it will be - - - s-i-o-n. Write these two possible spellings under the appropriate word.

direction   explosion
station   stasion

Tell your students to decide which one "looks right" to them and to write **only the one** they think is correct. When the students have decided which one looks right and have written this word in the correct column, have your students find the word in the dictionary to "prove they are right." Don't wait for everyone to find the correct spelling. As soon as anyone has found it, ask all your students to turn to that page and verify the correct spelling. If any of your students guessed wrong, have them erase the incorrect spelling and write the correct spelling. Cross out the spelling you wrote that is not correct and continue with another example.

For the first examples, choose common words that you think most of your students will instantly recognize which is the correct spelling. As you write each word, explain your thinking. "If it is spelled like *direction,* it will be *d–i–v–i–t–i–o–n* , but if it is spelled like *explosion,* it will be *d–i–v–i–s–i–o–n*."

direction	explosion
station	stasion
divition	division

After you have written the word both ways, ask your students to choose the one they think is correct and write only that one. When they have made their choice, have them find the word to prove they were correct and then fix any incorrect spellings. Cross out your incorrect spelling.

direction	explosion
station	~~stasion~~
~~divition~~	division

Continue to add words and have your students guess and then check. As the lesson goes on, they should get quicker at finding the words in the dictionary.

direction	explosion
station	~~stasion~~
~~divition~~	division
lotion	~~losion~~
~~mantion~~	mansion

Continue to add words, including some words that are less common. If students protest that they don't know which spelling is correct, tell them to make a guess and that they have a 50-50 chance of guessing right! Don't allow them to check the dictionary until they have committed themselves.

direction	explosion
station	~~stasion~~
~~divition~~	division
lotion	~~losion~~
vacation	~~vacasion~~
~~mantion~~	mansion
~~televition~~	television
attention	~~attension~~
explanation	~~explanasion~~
~~extention~~	extension
contraction	~~contracsion~~
relaxation	~~relaxasion~~
condition	~~condision~~

At the end of the lesson, discuss with the students that just as some rhymes have two spelling patterns, so do some common endings. If they are not sure which spelling is correct, they should write it both ways and see which one looks right. If they are still not sure, they should use the dictionary and find the correct spelling.

Here are some words you might use to do *What Looks Right?* lessons for *er-or* and *able-ible*.

swimmer	governor	valuable	flexible
singer	~~singor~~	portable	~~portible~~
~~sailer~~	sailor	~~sensable~~	sensible
~~tracter~~	tractor	lovable	~~lovible~~
painter	~~paintor~~	miserable	~~miserible~~
computer	~~computor~~	~~terrable~~	terrible
~~conducter~~	conductor	washable	~~washible~~
remainder	~~remaindor~~	comfortable	~~comfortible~~
producer	~~producor~~	~~horrable~~	horrible
prisoner	~~prisonor~~	favorable	~~favorible~~
~~editer~~	editor	reasonable	~~reasonible~~
~~collecter~~	collector	dependable	~~dependible~~
drummer	~~drummor~~	~~convertable~~	convertible
gardener	~~gardenor~~		
employer	~~employor~~		

Word Parts Taught in These 25 Words

This chart shows what these 25 words should help your students understand about how prefixes and suffixes change meaning or how a word can be used in a sentence. Two "unpeelable" prefixes are included in this list. When you peel off the prefixes *de* and *ex*, there is no known word left. You may want to tell students the meanings of *de* and *ex* but for most students, *de* and *ex* will be chunks that help them pronounce and spell words but do not help develop meaning.

Word part	Key word	Change in meaning or how used	Spelling change	Type
mis	misunderstood	wrongly or badly		prefix
pre	preview	before		prefix
inter	intersection	between or together		prefix
under	underground	under or less		prefix
over	overweight	over or too much		prefix
or	governor inventor inspector	person		suffix
ible	flexible	able to		suffix
anti	antibiotics	against or opposed to		prefix
ive	protective defective sensitive effective creative	adjective	drop e	suffix
de	defend defense defensive	down or away		prefix
ive	defensive	adjective		suffix
ex	explode explosion explosive	out		prefix

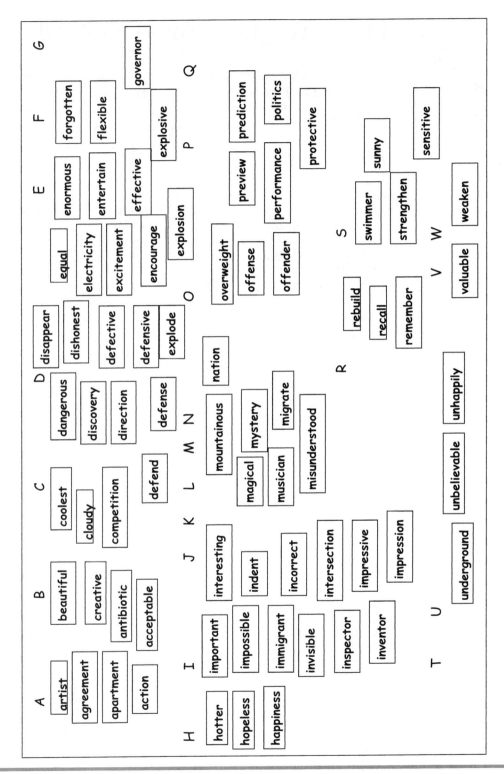

Word part	Key word	Change in meaning or how used	Spelling change	Type
im	impression impressive	in		prefix
ive	impressive explosive	adjective		suffix
ion	impression explosion	noun		suffix

Review, Consolidate, Celebrate!

The 75 words on your word wall and your students' growing ability to spell big words based on their knowledge of morphemic patterns have now empowered your students to spell over 700 words! Take a week or two off from adding words and use *Be a Mind Reader, Ruler Tap, WORDO, What's My Rule? Odd Man Out, Analogies,* and *Sentence Challenge* to review the word wall words and the words they generate.

The Last 25 Big Words and Their Parts

● Add 5 More Words

Only 25 words to go and you will have all 100 magic big words on your wall! The next 5 words to add to your wall are:

complete   composition   command   conclude   continue

All these words begin with the prefix *com* or *con,* which means "with or together." Unfortunately, we can't add this meaning to the other parts of the word because the root word is often a Greek or Latin word that most people don't know the meaning of. Prefixes *com* and *con* don't add meaning to most words but they are reliable spelling chunks and many words—*company, community, contestant, construction*—begin with these chunks.

Talk about the meaning of each word and then lead your students to cheer the words:

"complete c-o-m---p-l-e-t-e; c-o-m---p-l-e-t-e; c-o-m---p-l-e-t-e; complete"

"composition c-o-m---p-o-s-i---t-i-o-n; c-o-m---p-o-s-i---t-i-o-n; c-o-m---p-o-s-i---t-i-o-n; composition "

"command c-o-m---m-a-n-d; c-o-m---m-a-n-d; c-o-m---m-a-n-d; command"

"conclude c-o-n---c-l-u-d-e; c-o-n---c-l-u-d-e; c-o-n---c-l-u-d-e; conclude"

"continue c-o-n---t-i-n-u-e; c-o-n---t-i-n-u-e; c-o-n---t-i-n-u-e; continue"

After cheering for the words, have your students write each word.

complete

composition

command

conclude

continue

On the following day, lead your students to once again cheer and write the new words.

For the next several days, choose any 5 of the 80 words and have your students quickly cheer and write these 5 words. Then have them spell other words that can be spelled using the parts of the word wall words and other words they can spell. Be sure to talk about spelling changes before any words are written and how word parts change the meaning of the root word.

combat	commander	commandment	completely	completion
compose	composer	compound	compute	computer
conclusion	conclusive	confess	confession	consent
contest	continual	continually	continuous	continuously
contract	control	convert	discontinue	incomplete
incompletely	inconclusive			

● Add 5 More Words

The next five words to add to your wall are:

exports   exploration   destroy   destruction   delicious

The prefixes *ex* and *de,* like *com* and *con,* are added to Latin and Greek roots that we often don't know the meaning of. *Ex* means "out or away from." We ship *exports* out of the country. *Explorers* go out to places they have never been to before. *De* can sometimes indicate "an opposite meaning." *Defense* is the opposite of *offense. Destruction* is the opposite of *construction.* In many words, such as *delicious, de* is just a spelling chunk.

Lead your students to cheer the words:

"exports e-x-p-o-r-t-s; e-x-p-o-r-t-s; e-x-p-o-r-t-s; exports"

"exploration e-x---p-l-o-r---a-t-i-o-n; e-x---p-l-o-r---a-t-i-o-n; e-x---p-l-o-r---a-t-i-o-n; exploration"

"destroy d-e---s-t-r-o-y; d-e---s-t-r-o-y; d-e---s-t-r-o-y; destroy"

"destruction d-e---s-t-r-u-c---t-i-o-n; d-e---s-t-r-u-c---t-i-o-n; d-e---s-t-r-u-c---t-i-o-n; destruction"

"delicious d-e-l-i-c-i-o-u-s; d-e-l-i-c-i-o-u-s; d-e-l-i-c-i-o-u-s; delicious"

After cheering for the words, have your students write each word.

exports

exploration

destroy

destruction

delicious

On the following day, lead your students to cheer and write the new words once more.

For the next several days, choose any 5 of the 85 words and have your students quickly cheer and write these 5 words. Then have them spell other words that can be spelled using the parts of the word wall words and other words they can spell. Be sure to talk about spelling changes before any words are written and how word parts change the meaning of the root word.

construction	constructive	decompose	define	definition
deflate	defrost	defroster	degrees	delight
delightful	demand	department	depend	describe
desirable	desire	destroyer	destructive	exact
exactly	exam	excuse	exit	expiration
expire	explore	explorer	exportable	exportation
exporter	expose	exposition	gracious	importation
importer	indestructible	overexposed	spacious	suspicious
underexposed	undesirable	unexcused	unexplored	

● Add 5 More Words

The next five words to add to your wall are:

promotion   produce   production   information   transfer

Pro is a prefix that can mean "for or forward." When you are *promoted* to the next grade you are moved forward. *Produce* means "to make something." Computer factories *produce* computers. The producer *produces* the movie and we call this movie a *production*. *Information* is knowledge—facts and figures. When we have a lot of *information,* we are informed. *Transfer* begins with the prefix *trans,* which can mean "across." The *transcontinental* railroad goes across the continent. *Transmitters* send signals across many miles. Many words that begin with *pro* or *trans* are based on Latin or Greek roots. Although *pro* and *trans* don't often help us with the meaning of words, they are reliable spelling chunks.

Lead your students to cheer the words:

"produce p-r-o---d-u-c-e; p-r-o---d-u-c-e; p-r-o---d-u-c-e; produce"

"production p-r-o---d-u-c---t-i-o-n; p-r-o---d-u-c---t-i-o-n; p-r-o---d-u-c---t-i-o-n; production"

"promotion p-r-o---m-o-t-i-o-n; p-r-o---m-o-t-i-o-n; p-r-o---m-o-t-i-o-n; promotion"

"information i-n-f-o-r-m---a-t-i-o-n; i-n-f-o-r-m---a-t-i-o-n; i-n-f-o-r-m---a-t-i-o-n; information"

"transfer t-r-a-n-s---f-e-r; t-r-a-n-s---f-e-r; t-r-a-n-s---f-e-r; transfer"

After cheering for the words, have your students write each word.

produce

production

promotion

information

transfer

On the following day, lead your students to again cheer and write the five new words.

For the next several days, choose any 5 of the 90 words and have your students quickly cheer and write these 5 words. Then have them spell other words that can be spelled using the parts of the word wall words and other words they can spell. Be sure to talk about spelling changes before any words are written and how word parts change the meaning of the root word.

conform	conformist	deform	formal	formally
inform	informal	informally	informative	informer
introduce	introduction	platform	producer	productive
progress	progression	progressive	prolong	promote
promoter	proposal	propose	protest	provide
provision	reduce	reduction	refer	remote
remotely	reproduce	reproduction	transform	transformation
transformer	translate	translation	transmit	transmitter
transplant	transport	transportation	uninformed	unproductive

● Add 5 More Words

The next five words to add to your wall are:

confident   confidence   different   independent   nonviolent

If you are *confident* you can do something, you have a lot of *confidence*. Notice the spelling change from a *t* to a *c*. How would you spell *difference? Independence?* The prefix *non* often means "none." If a demonstration or protest is *nonviolent,* there should not be any violence.

Lead your students to cheer the words:

"confident c-o-n---f-i-d-e-n-t; c-o-n---f-i-d-e-n-t;
c-o-n---f-i-d-e-n-t; confident"

"confidence c-o-n---f-i-d-e-n-c-e; c-o-n---f-i-d-e-n-c-e;
c-o-n---f-i-d-e-n-c-e; confidence"

"different d-i-f-f-e-r---e-n-t; d-i-f-f-e-r---e-n-t; d-i-f-f-e-r---e-n-t; different"

"independent i-n---d-e-p-e-n-d---e-n-t;
i-n---d-e-p-e-n-d---e-n-t; i-n---d-e-p-e-n-d---e-n-t; independent"

"nonviolent n-o-n---v-i-o-l-e-n-t; n-o-n---v-i-o-l-e-n-t;
n-o-n---v-i-o-l-e-n-t; nonviolent"

After cheering for the words, have your students write each word.

confident

confidence

different

independent

nonviolent

On the following day, have students explain the relationships and spelling changes for the words and lead them to again cheer and write the new words.

For the next several days, choose any 5 of the 95 words and have your students quickly cheer and write these five words. Then have them spell other words that can be spelled using the parts of the word wall words and other words they can spell. Be sure to talk about spelling changes before any words are written and how word parts change the meaning of the root word.

absence	absent	dependable	dependably	dependence
dependent	difference	independence	independently	interdependence
interdependent	nonfat	nonliving	nonsense	nonstop
nonviolence	overconfidence	overconfident	silence	silent
undependable	violence	violent		

● Add 5 More Words

The final five words to add to your wall are:

adventure   signature   design   classify   identification

The words *adventure* and *signature* both end with the suffix *ture*. The words *signature* and *design* both contain the Latin root sign that means a mark or shape that has a particular meaning. What do the equal signs in math mean? What does a stop sign mean? What is sign language? When you sign something with your *signature,* you are putting your particular mark on it. When you *design* something, you are deciding its shape or form. When you *classify* things, you put the things that are alike together. Things that are classified together are in the same class or classification. If there is a robbery and you identify the robbers, we say you have made an *identification.*

Lead your students to cheer the words:

"adventure a-d-v-e-n---t-u-r-e; a-d-v-e-n---t-u-r-e; a-d-v-e-n---t-u-r-e; adventure"

"signature s-i-g-n---a---t-u-r-e; s-i-g-n---a---t-u-r-e; s-i-g-n---a---t-u-r-e; signature"

"design d-e---s-i-g-n; d-e---s-i-g-n; d-e---s-i-g-n; design"

"classify c-l-a-s-s---i-f-y; c-l-a-s-s---i-f-y; c-l-a-s-s---i-f-y; classify"

"identification i-d-e-n-t-i-f-i---c-a-t-i-o-n; i-d-e-n-t-i-f-i---c-a-t-i-o-n; i-d-e-n-t-i-f-i---c-a-t-i-o-n; identification"

After cheering for the words, have your students write each word.

adventure

signature

design

classify

identification

On the following day, lead your students to talk about the meanings of the words and to cheer and write the new words again.

For the next several days, choose any 5 of the 100 words and have your students quickly cheer and write these five words. Then have them spell other words that can be spelled using the parts of the word wall words and other words they can spell. Be sure to talk about spelling changes before any words are written and how word parts change the meaning of the root word.

adventurous	beautification	beautify	capture	classification
classy	cosign	declassified	dentures	departure
designation	designer	electrification	electrify	fixture
fortification	fortify	fracture	future	identify
identity	justifiable	justification	justify	magnification
magnify	misadventure	misclassify	mixture	modification
modify	natural	nature	picture	purification
purify	ratification	ratify	recapture	reclassify
resign	resignation	restructure	signal	signer
signify	structural	structure	terrify	texture
torture	unidentified	unification	unify	unjustifiable

Word Parts Taught in These 25 Words

This chart shows what these 25 words should help your students understand about how prefixes and suffixes change meaning or how a word can be used in a sentence. Five "unpeelable" prefixes are included in this list. When you peel off the prefixes *com/con, de, ex,* and *pro,* there is no known word left. You may want to tell students the meanings of these prefixes but for most students, they will be chunks that help them pronounce and spell words but do not help develop meaning.

Word part	Key word	Change in meaning or how used	Spelling change	Type
com/con	complete composition command conclude continue	with or together		prefix
ex	exports exploration	out or away from		prefix
de	destroy destruction design	down or away		prefix
de	delicious			chunk
pro	produce production promotion	for or forward		prefix
tion	production promotion information	noun		suffix
trans	transfer	across		prefix
ent	different confident independent	adjective		suffix
ence	confidence nonviolence	noun	t to c t to c	suffix
non	nonviolent	not or without		prefix
in	independent	opposite		prefix
ture	adventure signature			chunk
ify	classify	to make		suffix
tion	identification	noun	y to ica	suffix

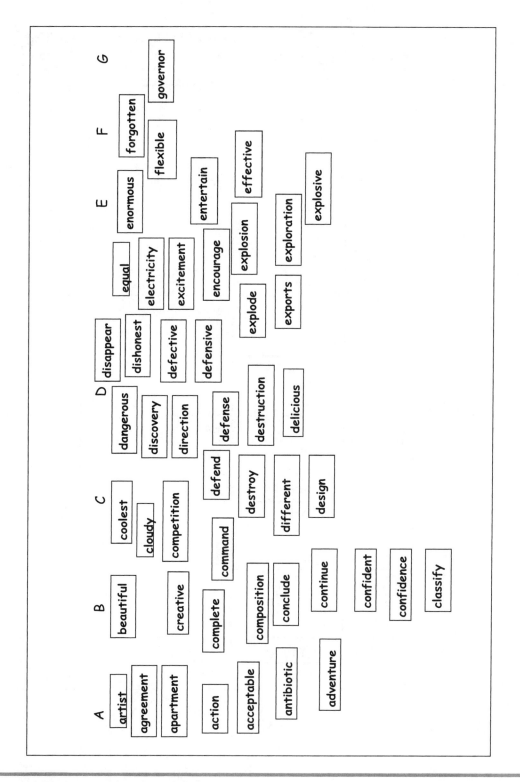

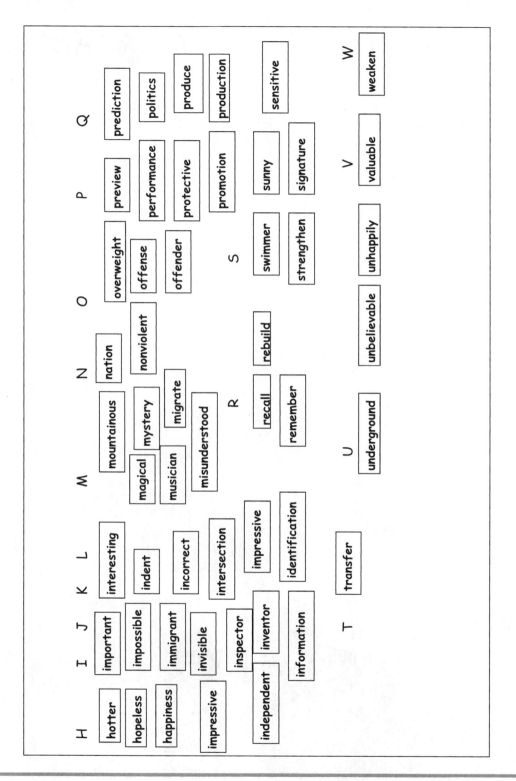

H
hotter
hopeless
happiness
impressive

I
important
impossible
immigrant
invisible
inspector
independent
inventor
information

J

K
indent

L
interesting
incorrect
intersection
impressive
identification

M
mountainous
magical
mystery
musician
migrate
misunderstood

N
nation
nonviolent

O
overweight
offense
offender

P
preview
performance
protective
promotion

Q
prediction
politics
produce
production

R
recall
rebuild
remember

S
sunny
swimmer
strengthen
signature
sensitive

T
transfer

U
underground
unbelievable
unhappily

V
valuable

W
weaken

Review, Consolidate, Celebrate!

The 100 words on your word wall and your students' growing ability to spell big words based on their knowledge of morphemic patterns have now empowered your students to spell over 1,000 words! Review the word wall words and the words they generate with games such as *Be a Mind Reader, Ruler Tap, WORDO, What's My Rule?, Odd Man Out, Analogies,* and *Sentence Challenge.* Challenge your students to write sentences using as many of the 100 words as possible.

Book Study Guide
for
What Really Matters in Spelling

Book Study Guidelines

Reading, reacting, and interacting with others about a book is one of the ways many of us process new information. Book studies are a common feature in many school districts because they recognize the power of collaborative learning. The intent of a book study is to provide a supportive context for accessing new ideas and affirming best practices already in place. Marching through the questions in a lockstep fashion could result in the mechanical processing of information; it is more beneficial to select specific questions to focus on and give them the attention they deserve.

One possibility to structure your book discussion of *What Really Matters in Spelling* is to use the Reading Reaction Sheet on page 246. Following this format, make a copy for each group member. Next, select a different facilitator for each chapter. The facilitator will act as the official note taker and be responsible for moving the discussion along. He or she begins by explaining that the first question is provided to start the group discussion. The remaining three questions are to be generated by the group. The facilitator can ask each person to identify at least one question and then let the group choose the three they want to cover, or the facilitator can put the participants into three groups, with each group responsible for identifying one question. The three questions are shared for all to hear and (and write down), and then discussion of Question 1 commences. The facilitator paces the discussion so the most relevant information for that group is brought out. Since many school districts require documentation for book studies, the facilitator could file the sheet with the appropriate person as well as distribute a copy to all group members for their notes.

Another possibility is to use the guiding questions for each chapter. You could have the same facilitator for all chapters. Perhaps this is someone who read the book first and suggested it to the group. Or the facilitator role could rotate. It is suggested that the facilitator not only pace the group through the questions to hit on the most important information for the group's needs, but also he or she should take notes for later distribution to group members and/or administrators if required for documentation.

The provided questions are meant to provoke discussion and might lead the group into areas not addressed in the questions. That is wonderful! The importance of a book study is to move everyone along in their understanding of the book content. If time is limited, the facilitator might select certain questions from the list for the initial focus of the discussion, allowing other questions as time permits.

Of course, a third option is to combine the two. Select the format that best fits your group and the time frame you have set for completion of the book.

All book sessions should end with a purpose for reading the next chapter. It could be to generate questions the group still has, to find implications for each person's own teaching, or to identify new ideas. Purpose setting is a time honored way to help readers (of any age) approach the text. If you are using the questions that accompany each chapter, direct participants to read the questions prior to reading the chapter. This will provide a framework for processing the information in the chapter.

Book Study Questions for Each Chapter

chapter 1: Spelling Matters

1. The book begins with the question, "Are you a good speller?" How would you answer that question? What experiences can you cite to explain your judgment about your spelling abilities?

2. Think back to your school years. What are your memories of spelling? Do you remember spelling lists and Friday spelling tests? Spelling bees? If you consider yourself a good speller, you may look back fondly on these traditional spelling events but you may view these same events differently if you are not a good speller. Discuss how traditional spelling instruction affects different students.

3. Ed Henderson was one of the pioneering researchers in the area of spelling. In 1985, he summarized his insights into spelling this way:

   > Those who set out to remember every letter of every word will never make it. Those who try to spell by sound alone will be defeated. Those who learn to "walk through" words with sensible expectations, noting sound, pattern and meaning relationships will know what to remember and they will learn to spell English.

   Think about the students you teach who struggle with spelling. Are they treating every word they meet as a new experience and trying to memorize every letter of every word? Do they spell words as if "wun leter ekwuls wun sond?" Unlike Spanish in which one letter does equal one sound, you have to pay attention to patterns of letters in English to be a good speller. Come up with a new word and ask your colleagues to guess how they think your neologism would be spelled. Discuss the spellings and see if you can determine which other words were used to construct a probable spelling.

4. To further complicate English spelling, some rhymes have two common spellings. Do your students misspell common homophones such as *sail/sale, right/write,* and *to/too/two?* Discuss with your colleagues how homophones create spelling problems for your students and what instructional strategies you have found to be effective for teaching homophones.

5. The author tells a true story in this chapter about a very bright boy named Scott who was quite a good speller but spelled *they t-h-a-y.* The probable explanation for this is that Scott was reading early and noticing how words were spelled by pattern before he had any spelling instruction. Because *they* is a very common word, he probably wrote it many times, spelling it like *may, day,* and *stay.* By the time he learned the correct spelling of *they,* his spelling of *t-h-a-y* was automatic, and when he was writing and not focusing on spelling, he spelled it in the way that had become automatic. Have you had similar experiences with precocious children who were reading and writing early? Discuss the problems that the common words that don't follow patterns—*they, said, was, have, friend*—present for you as you are teaching your students to spell.

6. The author presents three reasons why spelling matters. (a) Poor spellers do not like to write and often write as little as possible. (b) Noticing a word's spelling helps you remember the meaning for that word. (c) Spelling ability is closely linked to word identification. Discuss your students who struggle with spelling. Are they also your reluctant writers? Do they have fewer words in their meaning vocabularies than your good spellers? Do they also experience difficulty decoding new words they encounter in their reading?

7. Generate a question this chapter caused you to wonder about. Bring it to the group for discussion.

chapter 2: Building and Using a Classroom Word Wall

1. What is your experience with word walls? Have you ever had one in your classroom? Did you use the word wall to teach spelling? Was the word wall mostly room decoration? Share your experiences, successes, and problems with word walls.

2. It is often difficult to find just the right space in the classroom for a word wall. It needs to be where everyone can see it when they are writing and you need to choose a space that can be dedicated to the word wall for the entire school year. Discuss where you could put a word wall in your classroom. Can you think of other creative ways to solve the word wall space problem?

3. Cheering the words and writing the words are the two ways the author suggests for providing daily practice with the word wall. Think about what you know about learning styles and multiple intelligences. Discuss how cheering and writing the words supports the different ways your class full of individuals learn best.

4. We tell our students that the word wall is where we put the most important words—the words we all need to learn to read and spell quickly and automatically. Many teachers begin their word walls by gradually adding the names of the students in this class. Discuss how your students would react to having everyone cheering and writing their names. How might having their names there affect their attitude toward the word wall and toward spelling?

5. The author refers to Scott once again in explaining why you have to enforce the word wall rule: "If it's on the word wall, it has to be spelled correctly in everything you write." Your students who have some words they have been spelling automatically wrong won't be very happy to get papers back with a WW next to some words. You can quell their ire to some extent if you explain to them about how your brain works and how it makes things automatic once you have done them over and over. Think of some examples of automatic actions your students have learned—perhaps related to sports or riding a bike—and discuss how you would explain this automatic brain functions to students.

6. Generate a question this chapter caused you to wonder about. Bring it to the group for discussion.

chapter 3: Teaching the 100 Most Common Words and Patterns

1. The chapter begins by citing three research studies that demonstrate that improving your students' spelling will result in their writing more and with greater fluency. Think about your good spellers and your poor spellers. If these research studies had been done in your classroom, would they have gotten the same results?

2. The 100 words taught in this chapter are the most important words for beginners to learn to spell and read because they are the most frequently encountered words and contain examples for the most common patterns. Look at the total list of 100 words (pp. 58–61) and decide if you think these are the most useful words for your beginning readers. Are there any critical words you would add to this list?

3. Approximately half of the 100 words contain common rhyming patterns that should enable your students to spell many other rhyming words. The author included only rhyming words she thought might be in the meaning vocabularies of beginning readers. But, as the author points out, you are the expert on your kids. Look at the rhyming words generated and discuss with your colleagues any words you think most of your students would not have any meaning for. Make a list of words you would not use in the rhyming activities because their meaning would not be known.

4. These 100 words are appropriate and needed by most first-grade classes. If you teach older children, the author includes short paragraphs you can dictate to your students to see if they need to learn these words or patterns. Many teachers of older students find that their students can spell the common words such as *play* but are not able to transfer this to spell rhyming words such as *clay* and *stray*. If you teach older children, look at the diagnostic paragraphs and try to predict how well your students will do with them. Then use the paragraphs with your students and see if your predictions about their abilities to spell using rhyming patterns from familiar words were correct.

5. Generate a question this chapter caused you to wonder about. Bring it to the group for discussion.

chapter 4: More Common Patterns and Words Including Common Contractions and Homophones

1. The 100 words taught in this chapter include the remaining high-frequency words and common rhyming patterns. Combined with the 100 words taught in the previous chapter, if your students can spell these words as well as words with the same rhyming pattern, they should be able to spell a huge percentage of the short words they use in writing. Look at the total list of 100 words taught in this chapter (pp. 111–115) and the words taught in the previous chapter (pp. 58–61). Decide if you think these are the most useful words for your developing readers. Are there any critical words you would add to this list?

2. This chapter also teaches the spelling changes needed when *s, ed,* and *ing* endings are added to words. Becoming automatic with these spelling changes is quite difficult for many children. Discuss the instruction and practice activities this chapter describes to help your students become automatic at making these spelling changes as they write. How effective will these activities be with your students? Can you think of other activities that would help your students become automatic with spelling changes?

3. Capitalization is another spelling skill focused on in this chapter. Students learn key words for people, places, and holidays, and learn that they don't capitalize the general term—street, school, holiday, and others—but they do capitalize the specific names of people, places, and holidays. This is another complex skill that is difficult for many children to apply automatically as they write. How effective do you think the capitalization activities in this chapter will be with your students? Can you think of other activities that would help your students become automatic with capitalizing people, place, and holiday names?

4. Another spelling skill that presents difficulties for many children is to learn the spellings and meanings for common homophones. When homophones are taught, clues to meaning are attached to all but one of them. Students learn to determine if the spelling they are trying works with the clue and if not to use the other one.

Evaluate how effective you think this homophone instruction will be with your students and discuss other homophone activities that you have used successfully.

5. These 100 words are appropriate and needed by many second-grade classes. If you teach older children, the author includes short paragraphs you can dictate to your students to see if they need to learn these words or patterns. Many teachers of older students find that their students can spell common words but do not show in their writing that they are automatic with spelling changes, capitalization, and common homophones. If you teach older children, look at the diagnostic paragraphs and try to predict how well your students will do with them. Then use the paragraphs with your students and see if your predictions about their abilities to spell using rhyming patterns from familiar words were correct.

6. Generate a question this chapter caused you to wonder about. Bring it to the group for discussion.

chapter 5: Developing a Visual Checking Sense

1. Once your students are spelling by pattern rather than in a one-letter–one-sound way, they need to develop a visual checking sense. When reading, good readers are constantly monitoring by asking themselves, "Does this make sense?" When writing and spelling a less common word, writers need to ask themselves, "Does this look right?" To develop your students' visual checking sense, the author suggests doing regular *What Looks Right?* lessons. Discuss with your colleagues this lesson format and how your students would benefit from participating in some of these lessons.

2. As part of a *What Looks Right?* lesson, students use the dictionary to find the correct spelling of each word. To use a dictionary to find the spelling of a word, you have to have a few possible spellings in mind. How capable are your students at using dictionaries and how would the *What Looks Right?* lessons make them more independent spellers?

3. This chapter finishes the instruction in this book on capitalizing specific nouns by providing key words for months and places. How well do your students capitalize specific nouns in their writing? Evaluate the activities is this chapter for teaching capitalization.

4. Homophones are also a major feature of this chapter. The author suggests that you put a clue on all but one of the homophones to help students determine which word has which meaning, and that students might enjoy creating a homophone class book with the homophones taught in this chapter and with other common homophones. Discuss how your students would respond to these homophone activities. Are there any other homophone teaching activities other teachers in your group have used successfully?

5. Generate a question this chapter caused you to wonder about. Bring it to the group for discussion.

chapter 6: Building Meaning, Phonics, and Spelling for Big Words

1. Big words present particular spelling challenges for many older students. At the beginning of this chapter the author states, "In order to become a good speller from fourth grade on, you must abandon a 'memorize the letters' strategy or a 'write down the letters that stand for the sound' strategy and realize that even those patterns that work in short words often don't work in longer words. You need to develop a strategy in which you consider at some level what words might be related to this word." Discuss the examples given of morphemic links between words and come up with some other sets of morphemically linked words. How well do older students in your school understand the morphemic relationships words share?

2. Were you surprised to learn that 57 percent of all words that begin with prefixes begin with *un, re, in,* or *dis* and that only 20 prefixes, including these four, are found at the beginnings of all prefixed words? Students who know the meanings and spellings for these 20 prefixes gain enormous power with multisyllabic words. Look at the Prefixes, Suffixes, and Chunks chart on pages 172–176. Brainstorm some big words your students may not know the meaning of but whose meaning they could quickly figure out if they applied their knowledge of these prefixes.

3. Just as there are not a lot of prefixes to learn, there are also not a lot of suffixes. Suffixes sometimes add meaning but more often change where a word can be used in a sentence. Look at the suffixes in the chart on pages 174–176. Brainstorm some words that knowledge of these suffixes would enable your students to understand and spell.

4. It is not just struggling readers who don't understand morphemic relationships between words. Research shows that achieving students often don't see these relationships when the pronunciation of the words changes (*sign, signal; origin, original*). Research also demonstrates that older students who are given instruction in morphology show gains in decoding, spelling, and meaning vocabulary. Discuss the students you teach and how you think the morphological instruction described in this chapter might increase their decoding, spelling, and vocabulary acquisition skills.

5. This chapter teaches 100 key words that serve as examples for all the common prefixes, suffixes, and spelling changes. The key words were chosen because they are known by most older students and thus can be the keys to unlocking other unfamiliar words. Talk about the list of words. Are there any that would not be known by many of your students? If any of the key words would be unfamiliar to your students, how could you build meaning for these words so they could function as key words?

6. Generate a question this chapter caused you to wonder about. Bring it to the group for discussion.

Reading Reaction Sheet

Facilitator/Recorder (person who initiated the discussion): _____

Group reactants: _____

_____

Date of reaction/discussion: _____

Chapter title and author(s): _____

_____

Question #1: What ideas and information from this chapter could be used in classroom instruction?

Reactions:

Question #2: _____

_____

Reactions:

Question #3: _____

_____

Reactions:

Question #4: _____

_____

Reactions:

References

Andrews, S., & Bond, R. (2009). Lexical expertise and reading skill: Bottom-up and top-down processing of lexical ambiguity. *Reading and Writing, 22*, 687–711.

Baumann, J. F., Edwards, E., Font, G., Tereshinski, C. A., Kame'enui, E. J., & Olejnik, S. (2002). Teaching morphemic and contextual analysis to fifth-grade students. *Reading Research Quarterly, 37(2),* 150–176.

Bear, D., Invernizzi, M., Templeton, S., & Johnston, F. (2008). *Words their way: Word study for phonics, vocabulary, and spelling instruction* (4th ed). Boston:Allyn & Bacon.

Berninger, V. W., Abbot, R. D., Abbot, S. P., Graham, S., & Richards, T. (2002). Writing and reading: Connections between language by hand and language by eye. *Journal of Learning Disabilities, 35*, 39–56.

Berninger, V. W., Vaughan, K., Abbott, R., Brooks, A., Abbott, S., Reed, E., et al. (1998). Early intervention for spelling problems: Teaching spelling units of varying size within a multiple connections framework. *Journal of Educational Psychology, 90*, 587–605.

Bosse, M.-L., Valdois, S., & Tainturier, M. J. (2003). Analogy without priming in early spelling development. *Reading and Writing: An Interdisciplinary Journal, 16*, 693–716.

Carroll, J. B., Davies, P., & Richman, B. (1971). *Word frequency book.* New York: American Heritage.

Clarke, L. K. (1988). Invented spelling versus traditional spelling in first graders' writings: Effects on learning to spell and read. *Research in the Teaching of English, 22*, 281–309.

Conrad, N. J. (2008). From reading to spelling and spelling to reading: Transfer goes both ways. *Journal of Educational Psychology, 100*, 869–878.

Cunningham, P. M. (2008). *Phonics they use: Words for reading and writing* (5th ed.) Boston: Allyn & Bacon.

Ehri, L. C. (1997). Learning to read and learning to spell are one and the same, almost. In C. A. Perfetti, L. Rieben, & M. Fayol (Eds.), *Learning to spell: Research, theory, and practice across languages* (pp. 237–269). Mahwah, NJ: Erlbaum.

Freyd, P., & Baron, J. (1982). Individual differences in acquisition of derivational morphology. *Journal of Verbal Learning and Verbal Behavior, 21*, 282–295.

Graham, S., Berninger, V., Abbott, R., Abbott, S., & Whitaker, D. (1997). Role of mechanics in composing of elementary school students: A new methodological approach. *Journal of Educational Psychology, 89*, 170–182.

Graham, S., Harris, K. R., & Chorzempa, B. F. (2002). Contribution of spelling instruction to the spelling, writing, and reading of poor spellers. *Journal of Educational Psychology, 94,* 669–686.

Henderson, E. H.(1985). *Teaching spelling.* Boston: Houghton Mifflin.

McCutchen, D., Green, L., & Abbott R. D. (2008). Children's morphological knowledge: Links to literacy. *Reading Psychology, 29,* 289–314.

Nunes, T., & Bryant, P. (2006). *Improving literacy by teaching morphemes.* London: Routledge.

O'Grady, W., Dobrovolsky, M., & Aronoff, M. (1989). *Contemporary linguistics.* New York: St. Martin's Press.

Rasinski, T., Padak, N., Newton, R. M., & Newton, E. (2008). *Greek & Latin roots: Keys to building vocabulary.* Huntington Beach, CA: Shell Education.

Rosenthal, J., & Ehri, L. C. (2008). The mnemonic value of orthography for vocabulary learning. *Journal of Educational Psychology, 100,* 175–191.

Shahar-Yames, D., & Share, D. L. (2008). Spelling as a self-teaching mechanism in orthographic learning. *Journal of Research in Reading, 31,* 22–39.

Templeton, S. (1991). Teaching and learning the English spelling system: Reconceptualizing method and purpose. *Elementary School Journal, 92,* 185–201.

Templeton, S. (1992). Theory, nature and pedagogy of higher-order orthographic development in older children. In S. Templeton & D. Bear (Eds.), *Development of orthographic knowledge and the foundations of literacy: A memorial Festschrift for Edmund H. Henderson* (pp. 253–278). Hillsdale, NJ: Erlbaum.

Treiman, R. (1998). Why spelling? The benefits of incorporating spelling into beginning reading instruction. In J. L. Metsala & L. C. Ehri (Eds.), *Word recognition in beginning literacy* (pp. 289–313). Mahwah, NJ: Erlbaum.

White, T., Sowell, J., & Yanagihara, A. (1989). Teaching elementary students to use word-part clues. *The Reading Teacher, 42,* 302–308.

Wylie, R. E., & Durrell, D. D. (1970). Teaching vowels through phonograms. *Elementary English, 4,* 787–791.

Zeno, S. M., Ivens, S. H., Millard, R. T., & Duvvuri, R. (1995). *The educator's word frequency guide.* Brewster, NY: Touchstone Applied Science Associates.